Eastern
Carols
Bell
Church Point
Elvina Bay
Elvina
Carrs Creek

ANGAUA,
LOVETT BAY,
VIA CHURCH

A LIFE ON PITTWATER

Susan Duncan

Photography by Anthony Ong

EBURY PRESS

CONTENTS

Author's Note

I have not attempted to write a history of Pittwater. All I wanted to do was try to record a little of the beauty of the landscape and the spirit of the community where I am fortunate enough to live. I would like to think that this book might become a small legacy to future generations. A beautifully photographed, unfluffed-up account of how we offshorers lived, loved, played and preserved our way of life, at a particular time. I fervently hope nothing intrinsic ever changes here, and that the pressure to develop as populations grow is resisted with force and, if necessary, fury. So that one hundred years from now, people will still be able to board the ferry at Church Point and disembark at Halls Wharf to take a walk through scrub, rainforest and the twisted vegetation of the escarpments. To see wallabies, goannas, a python or shy black snake or two, kookaburras and a blue sky littered with clouds of white cockatoos. What I hope more than anything, though, is that a century from now, no-one shakes her head in despair and says: 'Look at how they stuffed up.'

for the Pittwater offshore community – past, present and future

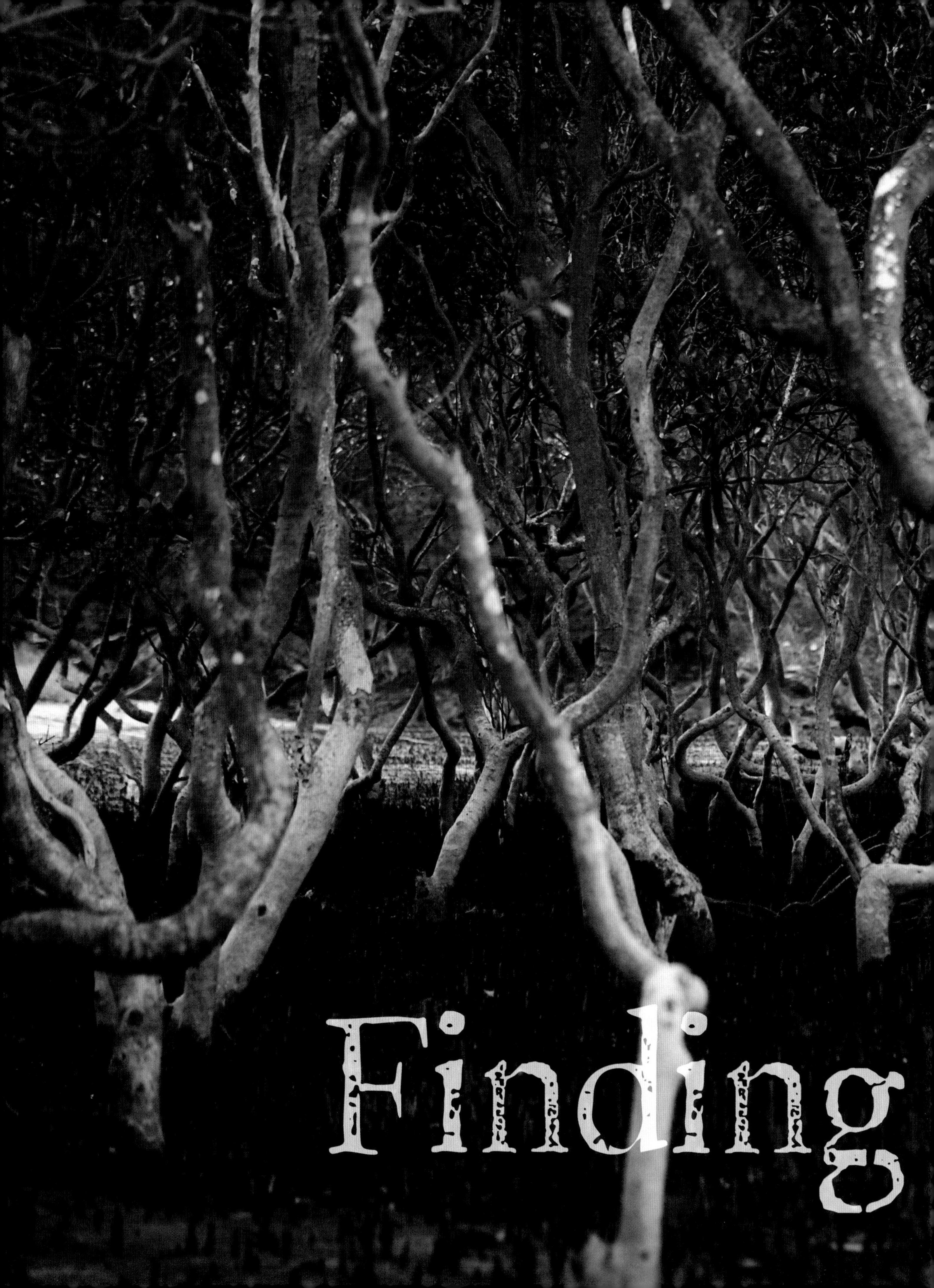
Finding

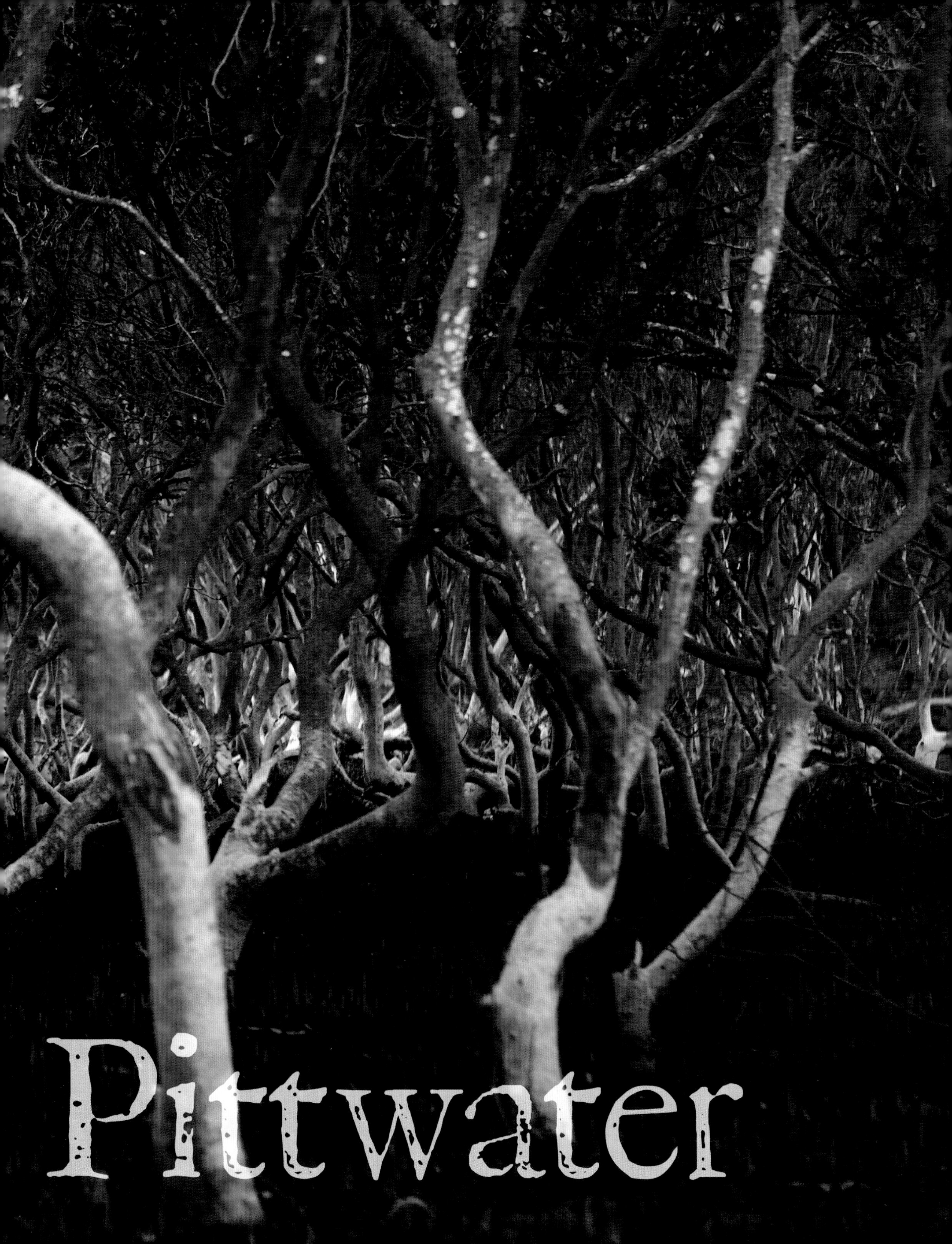

Pittwater

My first home on
Scotland Island, 1999

They say . . . when the wild beauty of Pittwater gets hold of your heart, it never lets go and you are seduced forever.

It is said that places find you – but only when the time is right. That was certainly true for me. The first time I saw Pittwater – a time I had all but forgotten – was in the early 1980s. I had recently returned from nearly a decade of living and working in New York as a journalist for Kerry Packer's Australian Consolidated Press. At the time, Sydney was new to me. I was born in country Victoria, raised mostly near Melbourne and had spent much of my adult life living and working abroad. The geography of Sydney's eastern and western suburbs was slowly becoming familiar but anywhere north of the Harbour Bridge was still downright foreign. I didn't have the faintest inkling a paradise such as Pittwater existed just a forty-five-minute drive from Sydney's CBD.

Journalist and author Neal Travis, who'd once been part of our small group of Australian expatriates working as foreign correspondents in the Big Apple, owned a basic fibro shack in Towlers Bay where a group of us were to stay for a weekend.

So we set off on an early spring Saturday morning, happy to have cast off the seedy, pressured claustrophobia of Manhattan for blazing blue skies, open spaces and the dry sting of a hot summer westerly. We were to meet four others at our destination. They had a boat to carry us on the last leg of our journey.

... the lovely old Curlew glides into Lovett Bay

to pick up passengers on the early morning run ...

... the tough, rugged, untamed bush
... the isolation and quiet ...

I must admit, I had very little interest in where we were going. I was thirty years old, madly in love with the man I soon married and I'd begun a job as a feature writer on a daily newspaper. Weekends were for food, fun and sleeping late. Where it happened didn't matter much.

I have hazy memories of that weekend: stepping on the gunnel of a rocky aluminium dinghy and nearly going overboard; nervously chugging through the water in a coughing, under-powered boat so over-burdened with people, wine and groceries, it's a miracle we didn't sink. I remember finally reaching an olive-green house with the dainty white flowers of potato vine spilling over the deck, thinking why would anyone want to live here where the only way in and out is in a small, unreliable tinny? I remember, too, the look of horror on my partner's face when he realised no-one had thought to bring potatoes.

'Someone will have to go back and get some,' he announced firmly and in a way that would have made his Irish ancestors proud. 'You can't have dinner without a few spuds.'

There was a collective sigh of relief moments later when a sack of rice was found in a kitchen cupboard. Yes, rice would do instead of potatoes, he nodded, as though a potential disaster of amazing proportions had narrowly been averted. No need for another perilous voyage.

But why, I wondered, would you want to live where even shopping for potatoes is a hassle? Looking back, I suspect I also felt threatened by the isolation and quiet, the ancient ochre escarpments that loomed behind us, the prickly bush, the deep green water. The reality of the bush, with its snakes, spiders, ticks, leeches, vicious scrub and every kind of unseen and lurking predator, actually scared me to death. I had grown accustomed to cities – taxis, restaurants, supermarkets, street lights. Even a dangerous town like New York, where nuts, bums and con men roamed the streets looking for prey, seemed a lesser menace than this wild shore from where there was no easy escape.

That night, as I lay in bed listening to the sound of water flopping on the shore in lazy breaking waves, I wondered about the emotional tug that had brought me home after so many years abroad.

A tug, I believed, that was a desire to be back amongst the red, blue, green, grey and gold landscape of my childhood.

But nostalgia was really the reason for my return, a dreamy and romantic yearning for the clean white light of summer days and softer winters without snow, sleet and slush.

A desire, too, to be back in a familiar world where there was no need to explain Bradman, Phar Lap, Bondi or Vegemite.

None of us ventured much further than the deck of Neal's shack that weekend and we left for the city after a long Sunday lunch and too many glasses of wine. Back where there were roads, cars and crowds. I crawled out of the tinny with relief.

My lingering impression of the weekend was the thought that I 'd like to grow the tough little creeper that emblazoned the crude shack with a delicate prettiness in a yard of my own one day. I didn't even bother to remember that the area was called Pittwater. And it was years before I learned that in the bush, potato vine *(solanum tuberosum)* was considered a weed.

I didn't return to Pittwater again until the mid-1990s, when I was invited to a friend's birthday party. I was newly widowed, retired and struggling to work out where I fitted in now that I was no longer anchored by a marriage or a career. This time I fell in love with the place and understood its unique beauty. I visited countless times over the next few years, arriving with joy for a weekend and leaving with a hankering to be back before I'd even stepped ashore. On gloomy city days, I found myself daydreaming of yachts under sail on glittering water, a great yellow moon brighter than dawn, the silvery softness of a flannel flower.

One traffic-filled, stressed day I asked myself a question: *If I could do anything I wanted, what would it be?* And the answer roared back: *Return to Pittwater and stay.*

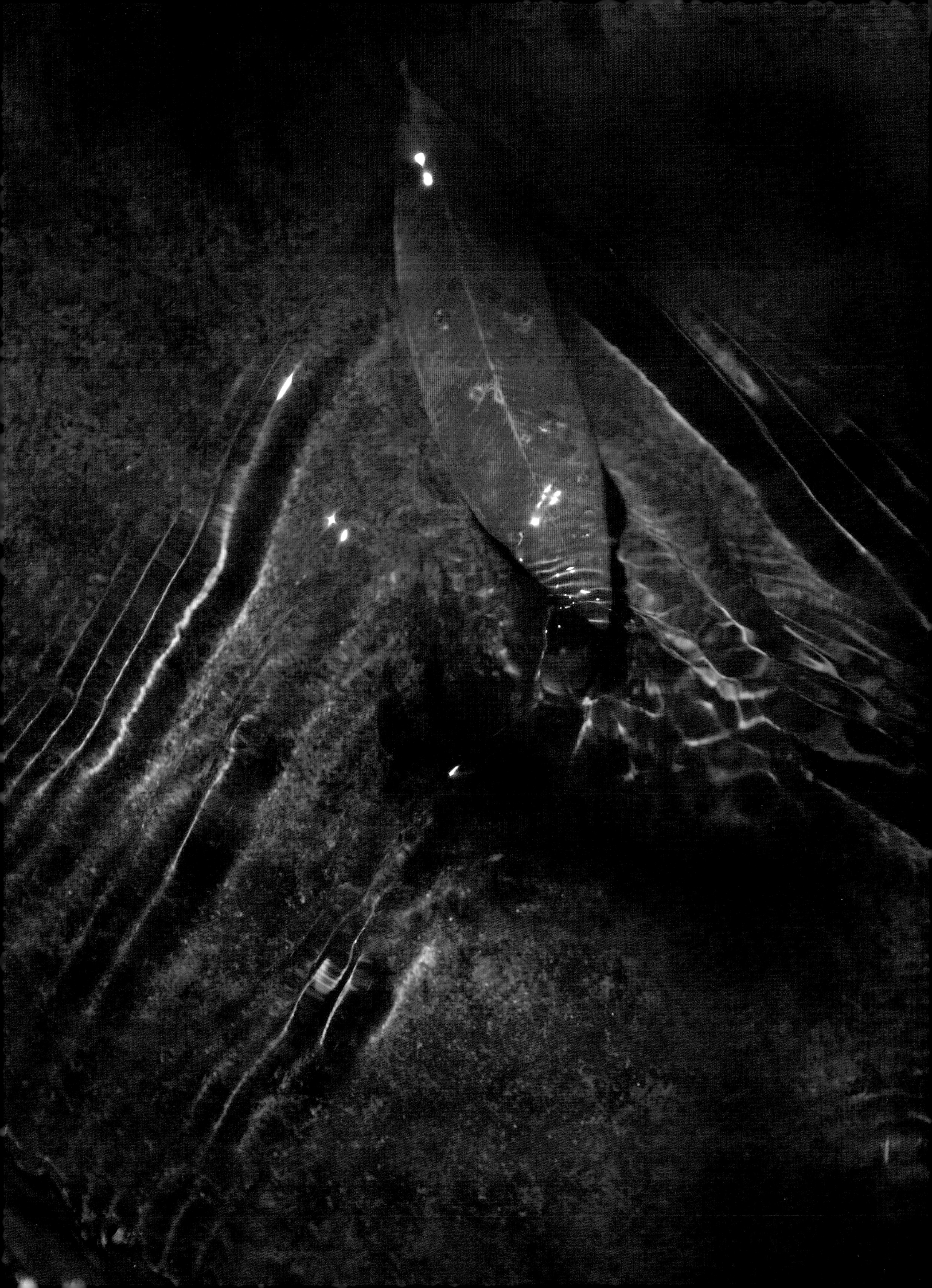

PITTWATER IS THE SOUTHERN ARM of a vast waterway that stretches from Broken Bay at the mouth of the Pacific Ocean, to end in a hand-spread of five bays reaching out from Scotland Island. The bays – McCarrs Creek, Elvina, Lovett, Little Lovett and Towlers (also referred to as Morning Bay) – are known as the Western Foreshores and are backed by the rugged Ku-ring-gai Chase National Park. Since European settlement, the area has been home to convicts, rum smugglers, madams, loggers and farmers. There was once a thriving salt business on Scotland Island and Aboriginal middens were burned to supply lime for the fast-growing colony of Sydney.

If it hadn't been for the foresight of an Englishman with the improbable name of Frederick Eccleston du Faur, the whole area would have succumbed to urban development long ago and one of the most pristine areas of native bush in Australia would have been lost forever.

Du Faur was a foundation member and trustee of what later became the National Gallery of NSW. He was so passionate about the natural world he joined the committee of the Australasian Association for the Advancement of Science, which helped to raise funds for Douglas Mawson's expedition to Antarctica. He was also a keen conservationist, long before it became fashionable or even an issue in most people's minds, and he could see Pittwater was under threat. In a report in *The Sydney Morning Herald*, dated 18 December 1894, he wrote:

... everyone dreams of sailing away
someday when the sea is smooth & blue ...

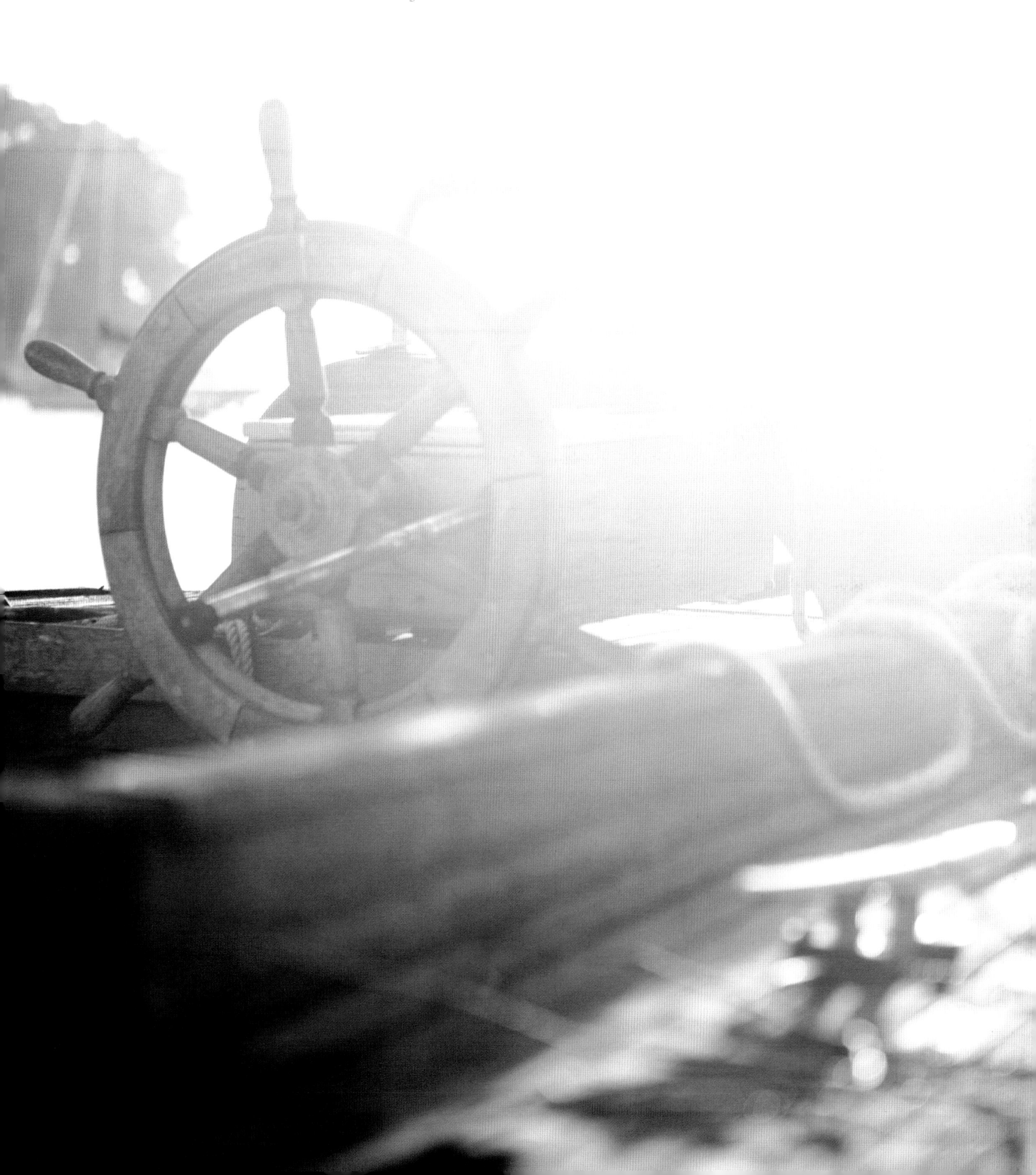

'The last tree ferns were being cut down, the rock lillies torn away by their roots and hundreds of Christmas bush trees of 50 years growth and upwards were being felled, merely to lop off branches for decoration of butcher's shops and other.'

Instead of allowing the area to be destroyed, du Faur believed it should be turned into a park on the same scale as Yellowstone in the US. He succeeded in pressuring the state government to set aside 35,300 acres from Hornsby to Pittwater, and bordering the waters of Cowan Creek and Broken Bay. Walking tracks, wharves and even a cottage at Towlers Bay were built to attract holiday-makers. All but the cottage still exists.

Over the decades, blocks of land along the shoreline were sold off to private owners for holiday homes. By the 1920s, a few grand houses were slowly appearing on the landscape. It wasn't until power was connected in late 1962 and phone lines hooked into individual homes instead of a single party line, though, that a few intrepid souls with a burning love for boats and water, for the freedom and isolation of the bush – as well as a desire to escape the confines of Sydney's cramped suburbs – began to live here permanently.

By the time I arrived in 1999 to rent a house near Bell Wharf on the western shore of Scotland Island, the area was a melting pot of artists, writers, publishers, engineers, architects, electricians, cooks, stonemasons, shipwrights, nurses, doctors, film makers, musicians, journalists, cleaners, builders, ferry drivers, odd-jobbers, retirees and an odd high-flyer or two.

I settled into a simple timber home so close to the water that it was wise to roll up the rugs on a king tide. It was a five-minute ferry trip from Church Point, the pick-up and drop-off point for most of the offshore community. Within weeks, I began searching for a home of my own.

Millpond-smooth waters before the sun comes up on the boatsheds of Lovett Bay.

... Pittwater was home to **convicts**,
rum smugglers, madams,
loggers and **farmers** ...

The Point

MINI-MARKET

General Store 2008 and right, 2009

Entering Pittwater, on the edge of the Ku-ring-gai Chase National Park, is like stepping back in time. In this ancient landscape, people commute by boat, wallabies graze on lawns, and goannas sneak in to steal a chicken off your kitchen table where you've left it to cool a little, before carving. There's often a python curled in the barbecue or a black snake lurking at your back door. Kookaburras swoop to lift a whole steak from your plate, and no-one finds it strange when you chase sulphur-crested cockatoos off your lemon trees at dawn, naked except for a tea towel.

For close to 200 years, the Western Foreshores were too isolated for any but the most adventurous – or the most reclusive – people to live, which is perhaps one of the reasons why such a strong sense of community remains today. On Pittwater, we are all interdependent. If you run out of petrol in a storm when you're crossing the bays, the first person passing stops to help. Otherwise, if the wind's blowing in the right direction, you could find yourself bobbing towards the great Pacific Ocean.

The central meeting place is Church Point, which is the ferry pick-up and drop-off point. It is shabby rather than swank, with a ramshackle general store that hangs over the water on crooked piles, a bottle shop, a few tables with bench seats and a scattering of shade trees.

GENERAL STORE
TAKE AWAY FOOD
SOUVENIRS
ICE & BAIT
HIRE BOATS
DECKSIDE DINING
Suitable identification must be produced in order to collect mail.
FAX SERVICE
RENOVATIONS NOTICE

POST OFFICE
CHURCH POINT 2105
ESTABLISHED 1ST JANUARY 1909

GENERAL
OST
FFICE
COFFEE
LOUNGE

Linger for a coffee, pick up the mail, have a chat at The Point while you wait for the ferry to take you home.

Nearly all we residents pass through regularly to pick up the mail, catch the ferry or on our way from the car park to our tinnies. It is a wonderfully successful and useful community gathering spot, perhaps because it has gently evolved since the earliest days of European settlement.

I think of it as our piazza or village square and can't help imagining, occasionally, that the spirits of long-dead residents still linger there with an occasional beer in hand and an ear cocked to hear any gossip.

At almost any time of the day, and sometimes late in the evening, you can find a kindred spirit for a chat and a catch-up. You can also organise an electrician, trade your lemon cake for homemade marmalade, talk through any issue before it escalates into a problem, or check out upcoming community events that are chalked on a nearby blackboard.

The General Store has a few gaping holes in the walls, salt-air damp has changed the shape of the windows so they barely close, and the floor never seems to be quite level. Inside, there's a mish-mash of odd, tacked-on corners for assorted uses. Fruit and vegetables along one wall. An alcove for washing dishes. A post office crammed into a space not much larger than a cupboard. Some dusty old shelves with sugar, flour, canned soup, detergent, dish cloths and a few other staples. There's a sign saying you can buy fishing bait but I never have.

A blackboard high on the wall above the takeaway food bar lists a menu of hamburgers, bacon and egg rolls, pies, sandwiches, cakes, tea and coffee. It's generally agreed that the hot chips are the best in Sydney and the crisp, fatty smell of them deep-frying on a chill winter evening weakens the resolve of even the strictest dieter. A scratched and ill-fitting rear door leads to a deck with tables, chairs and colourful umbrellas. Tourists and hordes of lycra-svelte weekend cyclists who find the challenge of steep and winding McCarrs Creek Road irresistible mostly use this area, and enjoy drinking coffee here while

Tie up the tinny, climb the ladder and order a bag of hot chips from the café.

the ferry comes and goes at the wharf alongside it. Most locals, though, opt for cheaper takeaway prices and carry their food to the square to eat with their legs hanging over the seawall while they throw a stick for their dogs.

Near the ferry office, which is no more than a timber shed with a desk, a chair and a phone, there's a tap with a huge water bowl so no dog ever goes thirsty. When a gorgeous old dog called Zeus was battling lung cancer and couldn't find enough breath to lap, someone attached a hose so water could be trickled down his throat. When Zeus died, there was universal sadness. Around Pittwater, dogs are as much a part of The Point – and life – as people.

It took a long time for his owner to finally find the heart to bring home a new puppy to keep him company on work sites around the bays.

A puppy that would ride the bow of his tinny and never stray more than a few feet from his side. Of course, the silky little tan and white pup was a ringer for Zeus.

Sometimes, if there's a rush on for coffee and hamburgers, the shy but genial postmaster, who remembers all our names and post boxes so even mail addressed to only a person and a bay finds the right home, can be found clearing tables or doing dishes. On frigid mornings, the water-taxi drivers slide behind the counter to warm their hands on the espresso machine. If anyone finds a set of keys, it's almost certain they'll be handed in. It is endlessly reassuring that these old-fashioned habits and values rarely falter.

... Commuter Dock, where we tie our tinnies
to go ashore, is a banging, clanging,
rocking and rolling mêlée
when the wind blows hard ...

A sprig of rosemary, a bugle call and the community remembers fallen heroes at the Anzac Day ceremony.

A large, plain building on one of the most beautiful slices of real estate in Sydney, dominates the eastern side of the square. Called the *Pasadena*, it was built in the 1920s as a Spanish-style hotel and restaurant. Now it's a popular spot for weddings and I've seen brides fly in by seaplane, or move slowly and regally by barge to the somewhat dodgy pontoon before walking along the jetty to take their vows on the lawn.

From the deck of my Scotland Island home, I sometimes watched the weddings through a telescope. I remember seeing one bride wearing a vivid orange wedding dress with glossy black feather trims at the hem and neckline. Her groom wore an equally iridescent orange suit and a black fedora.

Pittwater traditions, such as the Anzac Day ceremony and the shambolic but iconic Scotland Island to Church Point Dog Race, have sprung up around the erratically shaped little reserve with its seawall, sandy beach at low tide and views across the water. There is no better place to stand and sell tickets to community fundraisers, no better place to saunter when your own company begins to pall and you need to be reminded the world is bigger than whatever is bothering you. The Point has its own, inimitable spirit. It strengthens the links between the five bays and Scotland Island and ties us even more firmly together as a community.

… at almost any time of the night or day
you can find a kindred spirit
for a chat and a catch-up …

The routine for most of us is to pull into the drop-off bay at Commuter Dock to unload our shopping, which we stack neatly to one side at the end of the wharf. Then we leave it there while we park the car. The car park for offshore residents is located beyond the *Pasadena*. It is one of the few constant irritations in our idyllic life. Too many cars and not enough spaces sum it up. On weekends, you can circle for hours waiting for someone to give up a spot. Long weekends and public holidays are a nightmare. Tempers, normally sunny, fray and occasionally shatter if the day is sweltering, the chicken's going off, the ice-cream's melting and there's not a single damn spot left in the car park. It's amazing, though, how you can find ways to squeeze into the smallest space. I've seen people slam in their side mirrors, park within inches of the cars on either side, and then crawl out the back hatch in triumph.

Finding your car the next time you come ashore can be another problem. Did you park in McCarrs Creek Road or the car park? Or even up the hill behind the Church Point houses? It is quite common to see people wandering as though lost, *I could've sworn the car was here, or did David park it last?* Losing the car is not as ditzy as it sounds. If you plan well or don't have to commute to work, you can spend two or even three weeks without having to go ashore for supplies. That's when onshore life becomes a hazy memory while the reality of offshore living flows languidly along. Slow boat trips. Dinner with the neighbours. A bit of fishing if they're biting. A swim. A kayak. A yacht race. Whatever takes your fancy.

(Footnote: At the time of writing, the Pasadena *was scheduled for redevelopment and the General Store was undergoing extensive renovations. The new building, which has kept the spirit of the old, is pictured on page 27.)*

ALL SAIL
195721

Belonging

The Tin Shed,
Lovett Bay, 2007

Sometimes, if we are lucky, places find us and lead to joy, contentment and a glorious sense of belonging in a wondrous new world.

On a warm, late autumn day about five months after I began living on Scotland Island, I noticed a picture of a funny little house for sale in the local real estate office. For some reason – I will never know why because it was boxy, masculine and the antithesis of my flouncy dream home – I made an appointment to see it.

It was located in Lovett Bay and the agent, her assistant and I bumped across the water in an unstable, leaky tin dinghy for an inspection. It turned out to be a small, corrugated iron building, more like a shack than a home, with not even one of the features I thought essential – a deepwater jetty, winter sun, spacious rooms, two bathrooms and a glorious, whizz-bang kitchen.

I shook my head at the real estate agent. 'No, thank-you. Let's keep looking.' Then on a sudden whim, I made a silly offer, acting more out of pity than desire. The eighty-four-year-old owner, designer Gordon Andrews, once a muscled, irascible bloke who wore Levis and tight white T-shirts, had grown too frail to live on these isolated shores any longer.

I had no idea as we took our leave, putt-putting past an aloof and mysterious house tucked sedately into the side of a hill, that my offer would be accepted and I would tumble into a new life in a tiny waterside idyll where time seemed to stand still.

The battered pirate ship in Lovett Bay oozes the romance of the past, but now she rarely leaves her mooring and is home to nests of baby seagulls every spring.

The boatshed is a gathering point for neighbours who hang around catching up as the sun goes down.

We can never know, of course, what might have happened if we turned left instead of right at any given place at any given time in our lives. Or in this case, if my offer had been rejected. As it turned out, even though I initially thought I'd made the most expensive mistake of my life, in truth, I'd accidentally stumbled into where I truly belonged.

I discovered there was a waterfall in the south west corner of the bay that fell in foaming white torrents in heavy rain. Rainforests of rustling cabbage palms grew in the shelter of gullies, flanked by the rigid trunks of spotted gums, their roots splayed thickly like elephant feet in a bid to hold more tightly to precarious slopes.

A creek called Salvation fed into the estuary where white-limbed mangroves provided nurseries for fish to lay their eggs safely.

Near the ferry wharf there was a small beach of reddish sand where an elegant white-faced heron stalked prey with long-legged strides. Sinewy cormorants, swimming with their heads out of the water like periscopes, greedily scanned the water for baitfish. A pair of black ducks paddled by, looking for scraps. Sulphur-crested cockatoos shamelessly screeched from shore to shore, their pure white wings spread like kites. Beyond the beach, the coastline fell in a crumbled mass of sandstone. Slippery and beaded with seaweed and sharp-edged oyster shells.

LOVETT BAY BOAT SHED

... at dusk the sand flats turn
the colour of beaten gold ...

NB362N

Through the windows of my little shack, I could see boats swinging gently on their moorings. An old tug with a hull so svelte and sweeping, her beauty shone through the decay. The pirate boat, black and sinister. It's sunk once or twice, when the winds have howled into the bay bringing confused seas and torrential rain. But it is always raised again from the sandy bottom and the seagulls rebuild their nests amongst the rotting ropes, sails and timber, hoping the oyster-encrusted hull will stay afloat until the chicks are old enough to fly. The 'Fruit Box' (pictured left), with its crooked sliding aluminium windows and wooden French doors, made me smile whenever I looked at it.

There were gleaming yachts too, but it is always the wrecks that intrigue. Who trod their decks? Sailed them far and wide? What adventures have they known and survived? How did they end up in Lovett Bay? Will they be left to sink? Or will someone, old or young and full of dreams, take on the job of resurrection? It's not a futile hope because Pittwater encourages the dreamer in all we mavericks who come to live here.

It wasn't the easiest transition from city slicker to boatie and if I'd railed against the difficulties of offshore living from the beginning, there is no doubt I would have quickly sold and moved on, as some people do. Instead, I found I thrived on the challenge of docking boats in bossy winds. I was utterly seduced by nights spent sitting on the deck watching storms fling shards of blinding light through swollen skies. And even the untamed bush, framed by forbidding escarpments and an empty sky, eventually lost its threat as I learned to look intently enough to see its daily miracles.

New neighbours

Not long after I moved into what I soon came to call the Tin Shed, I met the couple who lived in the grand, mysterious house that presided over Lovett Bay with a quiet but firm presence.

Bob Story, an engineer, and his wife, Barbara, had moved from a conservative suburb on the Mornington Peninsula in Victoria, trading a hectic life of running a business and raising four children for a cosy but comfortably challenging retirement of sailing and exploring the bush.

Most people who come to live at Pittwater have a story to tell about moving day. Rain. Hail. Sleet. Blasting southerlies. Unhelpful tides. Furniture overboard. Sinking tinnies. Anything can happen when you're at the mercy of wind and water. For Bob and Barbara, though, it was almost catastrophe. On 9 January 1994, two weeks before their furniture was due to arrive from Melbourne, bushfires rampaged through the Ku-ring-gai Chase National Park. Like everyone else in the area, they'd been warned to stay away by authorities that threatened arrest if anyone disobeyed. They sat, helpless, at a Newport yacht club, watching and waiting while the sky turned blood orange.

By sunset on that day of horror, through the choking haze and heat, of leaves, branches and loose debris hurtling through the air in wicked westerly winds, it was impossible to tell where the water ended and the land began. Lovett Bay, they were told, had been hit hard.

That night, when not a single light shone from a house and the bays were pitch black,

a strong sea breeze kicked in and turned back the westerly. At dawn, Bob and Barbara boarded *Larrikin*, their 33-foot yacht, and slowly motored through a charred, still-smoking landscape, dreading what they might find. In the ashen light they slowly cruised past skeletons of houses, burning jetties, straining to see whether the home of their dreams remained standing. Surrounded by blackened trees and powdery grey earth, but still grand and powerful against the naked landscape, *Tarrangaua* had survived. Even the timber workshed escaped without so much as a singe.

As they motored beyond the house and closer to the estuary where Salvation Creek runs into the bay they saw nothing but devastation. The remains of four homes lay twisted and crumpled on the ground. Corrugated water tanks, their timber platforms devoured by flames, had collapsed. All that remained intact were a single, cast iron bathtub and the upturned dinghy on two poles that forms an arch across the jetty leading to the Lovett Bay boatshed.

Gordon Andrews, the man from whom I bought the Tin Shed, was the first to rebuild – at the age of eighty.

Bob and Barbara's priority, after they finally settled into their new home, was to train as volunteer fire fighters with the West Pittwater Volunteer Fire Brigade.

The day the fires raged through the bush, destroying homes, jetties and boatsheds in minutes.

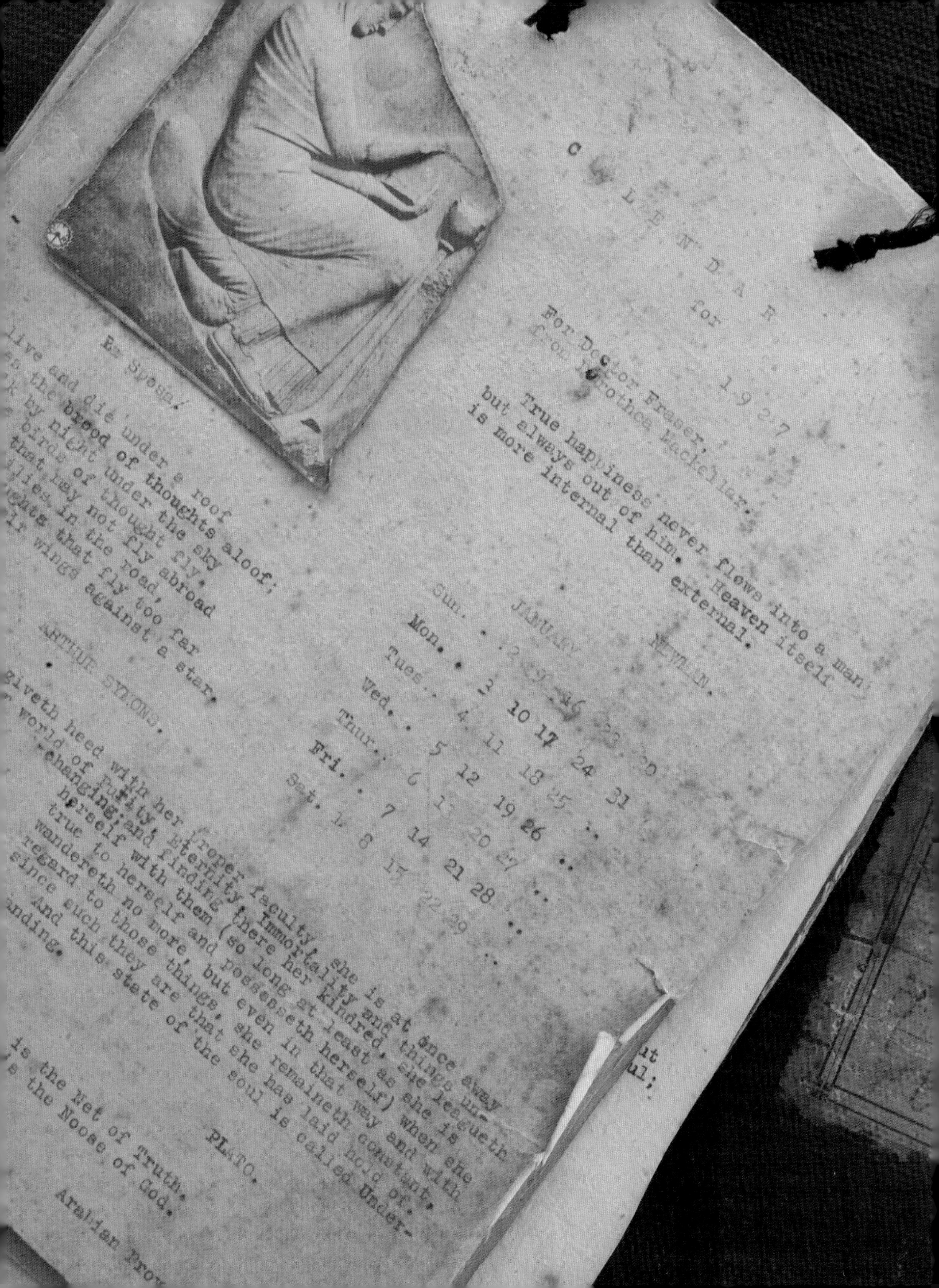

C L E N D A R
for
1927
For Doctor Fraser,
True happiness never flows into a man,
but always out of him. Heaven itself
is more internal than external.
NEWMAN.
JANUARY
Sun. . . 2 9 16 23 30
Mon. . 3 10 17 24 31
Tues.. 4 11 18 25 ..
Wed. . 5 12 19 26 ..
Thur.. 6 13 20 27 ..
Fri. . 7 14 21 28 ..
Sat. 1 8 15 22 29 ..
live and die under a roof
brood of thoughts aloof;
by night under the sky
birds or thought fly,
that may not fly abroad
lies in the road,
that fly too far
wings against a star.
ARTHUR SYMONS.
giveth heed with her proper faculty, she is at once away
world of Purity, Eternity, Immortality and things un-
changing, and finding there her kindred, she leagueth
herself with them (so long at least as she is
true to herself and possesseth herself) when she
wandereth no more, but even in that way and with
regard to those things, she remaineth constant,
since such they are that she has laid hold of.
And this state of the soul is called Understanding.
PLATO.
is the Net of Truth.
is the Noose of God.

The Poet

The Dawn of a New Civilization
By Hardy Wilson
PALMER
DOROTHEA MACKELLAR
Dorothea Mackellar

She was rich, reclusive and would have been forgotten but for a single poem that fired the imagination of a brave new world.

T*arrangaua*, an Aboriginal word meaning high, rough hill, was built in 1925 as a summer cottage for the rich and reclusive poet Dorothea Mackellar. Born in 1885 into a family of enormous privilege and wealth, she wrote three novels, one in collaboration with her lifelong friend, Ruth Bedford, and four books of poems, which were published between 1911 and 1926.

Although she travelled widely with her politician father, spoke five languages and moved in circles that included many famous and influential people, she lived a sheltered, chaperoned life until she was in her thirties, and never married.

Mackellar would probably have been all but forgotten with the passing of time except for one thing. She wrote a poem that captured the imagination of a brash young colony, a poem that was learned by heart by generations of Australian school children. Even today, more than a hundred years after its publication, the poem evokes an instant passion for a 'sunburnt country' and 'a wide brown land'.

The poem, 'My Country', made her famous and she was invited to recite it over and over throughout her life. More than anything else, it gave her a sense of achievement and the belief that long after the power and wealth of the Mackellar family had dissipated, she would leave a worthwhile legacy.

Miss Mackellar, as she was universally referred to, was forty years old when she bought 9 acres on the south-facing shores of Lovett Bay. She engaged the Sydney architectural firm of Wilson, Neave and Berry to design the house and it was generally understood by her friends and family that the most controversial of the three partners, Hardy Wilson (1881–1955), whom the poet knew socially, undertook the commission.

She wanted *Tarrangaua* to be a summer cottage, a retreat from the steamy heat of Sydney summers where she could peacefully indulge her passion for swimming, reading and the bush. The construction of the house would have been fraught with difficulties.

Building materials had to be barged in on high tides, then transported up a steep incline to the site near the peak of the hill.

More than sixty-thousand bricks, eight massive columns for the verandah, thousands of fragile Marseille terracotta tiles for the roof, and tons of tallowwood and Queensland maple for the floors and cupboards. The sandstone foundations were quarried on site and stonecutter's marks can still be seen in the remains of boulders near the shore. There was no electricity, no phone lines, and the ferry wharf was a simple, stone seawall with rough, oyster-encrusted steps that went under water at high tide. It was not an undertaking for the faint-hearted.

Dorothea Mackellar's letterpress, wax sealing set and tagged house keys remain in the house today, carefully handed from one owner to the next so the history stays intact.

No More Ghosts
Robert Graves

The only surviving details of designing the house are two undated drawings for the septic tank, numbered 16 and 17, which are held in the Mitchell Library. No-one knows what happened to the earlier drawings and plans – perhaps they were innocently burned by the school children who were hired to clean out the house after Mackellar died in 1968.

Some memorabilia of the poet's time at *Tarrangaua* remain in the house. The cast-iron letterhead embosser. Her personal seal with its tiny ladle to melt the wax. A few books, collected over time, with her bookplates inside. There's a calendar, too, that the poet created for the doctor who lived down the hill. It is filled with references to love and makes you wonder if she may have had a crush on him. A cigarette case and lighter in vivid green have her initials on them, although Dorothea Mackellar, I was told, gave up smoking when she was quite young. And there is a shawl made of black silk, heavily embroidered with flowers in pastel colours and with a long, glossy fringe as fine as hair.

Bob and Barbara Story, the third owners of *Tarrangaua* since it was first sold after the poet's death, regarded themselves as custodians of the house as much as of the poet's possessions.

Tarr

angaula

'There is a house on a high, rough hill that overlooks the tawny green waters of Lovett Bay. It is pale yellow, with three chimneys and a red tiled roof splattered with lichen ...' Salvation Creek

Shortly before I moved to my Tin Shed, Barbara became ill. 'These have been the best years of my life,' she said one day as we sipped tea and ate cake on the verandah. It was her way, perhaps, of telling me that she knew she was dying. She told me, too, that there was a lane connecting *Tarrangaua* to the Tin Shed. 'It's called Lover's Lane,' she said with a knowing smile.

I had no idea – how could I? – that one day I would live in the house on the high, rough hill. But Bob and I fell in love in the best of all ways. We became friends first as we helped each other through difficult times. As Barbara knew we would.

After Bob and I married, I insisted we live in my Tin Shed, so he rented *Tarrangaua* to tenants. One day, a couple of years later, I watched Bob make about six trips to his workshed to get tools and something inside me let go.

'Should we give your house a go for a while?' I asked him, handing him a cup of tea.

'It wouldn't bother you?' he said, trying not to look hopeful.

'No. Not anymore.' And I realised it was true.

...chooks roam free,
winding stone stairways and gothic chimneys...

The main, long sitting room is embraced by the sweeping verandah with its corridor of muscular columns.

The tenants, by then, were in love with the bay. So we swapped houses on a fine day in late spring in 2003. I had one stipulation. My furniture had to come with me or I would feel like a guest.

'Fair enough,' said Bob.

For a while, I felt overwhelmed by the quietly grand sense of *Tarrangaua*, and I wondered if I should trade my boat shoes and jeans for brogues and twinsets. Then common sense prevailed. A house is a house, no matter who once lived in it, and comfort comes first. Coffee tables are for feet. Wine glasses shouldn't have to come with coasters. Dogs, even visiting dogs, have equal (well, almost) rights to sofas and if you rise from your seat with clothes covered in fine white hairs, well, that's okay. Life is for living, not worrying about dog hairs.

On our walls we have linocuts of Pittwater by a friend, Katie Clemson, and artist David Preston. They hang alongside paintings by local artists, all of them friends. Their vibrancy lifts the sombre works from the 1800s that my mother gave me as gifts on momentous occasions – my fortieth birthday, my marriage to Bob.

As the current owners of *Tarrangaua*, we are honorary custodians of a growing collection of Mackellar artifacts given to us by people who knew her. The Buddhist nun, Adrienne Howley, who nursed Mackellar for the final eleven years of the poet's life, gave us the emerald green cigarette box and lighter. George Bennett, who once owned the Lovett Bay boatshed, kept the calendar that Mackellar hand-typed in 1927 for the doctor who lived down the hill. For many years, George and his wife, Thelma, also stored an old cane suitcase that belonged to Mackellar's brother, Malcolm.

The original keys, letterpress and sealing wax set have been gifted from one owner to the next. I bought one of Mackellar's brass and crystal inkwells at auction, along with a book of poetry by Patrick Chalmers called 'A Peck O' Maut'. Chalmers was the man she hoped to marry. Legend has it that her letter accepting the marriage proposal went astray when World War I was declared and Chalmers, thinking he'd been rejected, married someone else on the rebound.

a designers life
MARGARET PRESTON

The master bedroom is at the rear of the house, although Dorothea Mackellar preferred to sleep in the room I now use as my study (bottom right). At some stage, the original green timber shutters were replaced by panes of glass.

Australian pottery and old enamelware evoke an earlier era. The eggs were laid by our hens in their coop with its magnificent views across Pittwater.

TEA
The SLOW

Barbara matched this plate with broken pottery found in Mackellar's rubbish dump, which was exposed by the 1994 fires.

For us, the key to life in *Tarrangaua* is without doubt the long, columned verandah with its magical views of ancient red escarpments, trickling waterfalls and a bay that changes colour from deep green to vivid blue – and every colour in between – throughout the day.

In summer, I make up a cane bed at the eastern end, Bob slings a mosquito net over a frame that he hangs from the ceiling and we sleep with the sea breeze blowing softly on our faces. The chiming of a knocking halyard, like a cow bell, drifts from the bay. The sounds of wallabies thumping past on their well-worn tracks, the mournful hoot of a mopoke owl and the rustle of a bandicoot in the hydrangeas, are night music.

In winter, we close the windows against the frigid southerlies and light the fire in the sitting room. Outside, the smell of woodsmoke lingers on the cold layer of air in the bay. When storms muster behind the hills of Salvation Creek and Elvina Bay, we move onto the verandah to watch the wind fling branches through the air.

Sometimes, I cannot believe my good fortune, my fortunate life. 

…building **boats**, splicing ropes, fixing table legs and **mending** teapot spouts – anything's possible in Bob's **chaotic** shed…

15154
CURLEW
The Spirit

Long, languid summer days, relaxing in the cool waters of the Bays, putting our crab pots out at dusk, kayaking at dawn – the pleasures are simple but intoxicating.

Pittwater is a unique little paradise where even though its pleasures are simple – swimming, fishing, boating, food, a rich social life and a wondrous environment uncomplicated by the need for pocket money and malls – they are the greatest privileges of all.

Weekends revolve around fun, food, an unassailable spirit of goodwill, kids, tinnies, yachts and lovingly restored old timber boats that shine with the patina of age and the beauty that comes from living long and well.

There are, however, two main elements. The water, which makes us all interdependent. And the community. Rich, diverse, engaging, funny, irreverent, kind, occasionally infuriating but rarely interfering. While we may squabble here and there – and we do – the desire to forgive, forget and move on prevails. Gossip is generally benign and neighbours prefer to handle their problems over a beer or a cuppa. The unspoken, underlying bond between us all is severed only if someone consistently and arrogantly steps a long way over the boundaries of acceptable behaviour. Even then, it takes a long time before offenders are quietly subjected to a turned shoulder, a curt nod instead of a friendly chat, or the withdrawal of invitations to participate

Australia Day picnic on the Trump, *a working barge; and kids cool off when the school day is ended.*

in community events. Petty squabbling, anyway, fades to nothing when the day, fat with heat, ends in a fiery sunset and a cool breeze blows in from the south to refresh; when moonlight tiger-stripes the water. When the bay is tweaked with white caps, Pittwater reminds you, over and over, that we humans are here for a second and it is the land and sea that endures, sustains and must be protected. And nearly always, if life suddenly turns belly-up, even for your antagonist, if he or she needs support, the slate is wiped clean and the community gathers quietly to lend a hand.

Community is the constant heartbeat of offshore living and it is a fierce guardian of the fragile principles that make our small part of the world unique. We all strive to preserve the hallowed sense of stepping back into a slower, more gentle era when eccentricities were not just tolerated but encouraged.

Occasionally, I meet people who wonder loudly why no-one's ever bothered to build a bridge linking us to Church Point. 'It would make life so much easier,' they tell us.

WHARF
NO TIE-UP AREA

Commuter tinnies with bailing buckets, petrol containers and flaking paint have hulls beaten into strange shapes by banging against other boats and jetties.

Dogs ride the bows of boats like naval commanders … and putting on the Ritz – Pittwater style.

I tell them about a little film made by a group of locals as part of the H20 360° Scotland Island short film festival. It was called *The Bridge*.

'Honey?' the film begins. 'Honey, we need milk.'

Sighing, *honey* closes his computer, walks down the long stairway to the shore, climbs into his boat and heads for the General Store at The Point. He buys his milk, checks his change and realises there's not much left from five dollars, sighs and gets back in his boat. Halfway home, the engine stalls. A kayaker glides past and offers to help. 'No thanks, mate.' The paddling begins. He hits a yacht on a mooring. Falls in the water. It's winter and it's cold. Eventually he arrives home, shivering, his leather jacket dripping but with the milk intact. 'What happened to you?' asks his wife.

'There's got to be an easier way,' he replies in despair, and his eyes light up at the thought of … a bridge.

That night he dreams of this bridge. The ease of commuting stretches out in front of him. The swoosh of traffic is like music. He jogs along this magical, mythical bridge, sees the exits marked Bell and Carol (for Scotland Island wharves). Then he pauses and looks back the way he has come. High-rise buildings are crammed all over the island. There are no trees. Just building after building. Brick, hard-edged, and not a square inch of soil is left uncovered. The community association, SIRA (Scotland Island Residents Association) is a massive, ugly squat building on the foreshore with as much character as an RSL club. Island life is suddenly city life. And it's a nightmare, not a dream.

... boats, kids, dogs, sunshine,
and a community picnic at the beach ...

Hold tight to the Christmas tree so it doesn't fall overboard.

He wakes to birds, decks, trees, houses lightly imprinting the shore, then climbs into his boat with his toddler daughter and scoots across the water to The Point. No traffic, no crowds. Just a blue stretch of open waterway and a friendly wave from a passing neighbour. He's a happy man. 'There's no bridge!' he exults. 'No bridge.'

I ONCE MET A WOMAN on one of the bush tracks that wind from Lovett Bay to Towlers Bay. She wore a lipstick red swimsuit covered by even brighter red shorts and she'd stepped off the ferry to look around.

'So you have cars here,' she said, indicating the rough roadway.

'No,' I replied. 'Only fire trucks or vehicles from the National Parks and Wildlife.'

'So everyone travels by boat?'

'Yep.' It was a thought that puzzled her deeply. Did she think we were all mad? Or that I must be lying because roads were sensible and boats, at best, whimsical.

40

… Frog Hollow nestles in a quiet cove
with a cave where lyrebirds sing their hearts out …

Poling out of Elvina Bay on an ebb tide after putting out the crab pots.

'But this is not an island. It is mainland, yes?'

'Yes, but road access would have to be through the national park.'

'Oh, but it would be easier then, yes? Not so hard to live here.'

'Maybe. But we don't mind the effort if it means keeping cars away, preserving what we like to think of as our wild tranquillity.'

I could see my reply didn't suit her concept of a practical universe.

'But trucks are allowed if you are building a house.' She said it like an irrefutable fact.

'No. Materials are shipped by barge from Cargo Dock on Pittwater Road.'

'Oh, that's terrible,' she said, horrified. 'Terrible. What a terrible way to live.'

'No,' I said, 'it isn't terrible. It's magic.' But she didn't get it and I'm not sure she ever would.

To be fair, when I first bought the Tin Shed and decided to do renovations, the instinct to save a few dollars wiped out the desire to preserve what I most prized, what had survived so exquisitely because of its logistical difficulties, what had brought me here in the first place. I muttered darkly about the inconvenience and added expense of water transport. I quickly embraced the idea of changing the rules even though it would inevitably open a floodgate and turn our quietly charming, isolated little bays into just another crowded suburb.

The thing is, though, the community would never have let me get away with it. The community keeps us honest.

The

Boatsheds

LAMEROO

VAILALA

The Witt family camping onsite before the house was built

The Pledge

Many of the quaint little holiday shacks from the mid-1950s onwards remain around Pittwater, their rears perched on the shore, their front rooms built on piles so they hover over the water like a ship's stateroom. They are ramshackle and today, no council would ever approve their construction. Yet they are utterly gorgeous with their uneven floorboards, doors without locks and windows so warped they refuse to open. Or close. Perhaps because they are exquisite reminders of the days when holiday houses were for . . . well, holidays! Letting kids run wild and come in filthy from the beach without being yelled at, and not bothering to make beds or clean the bathroom until the last day. Or perhaps their appeal is their closeness to the water where – if you look closely enough – a fish, a turtle or a gimlet-eyed stingray might stare back.

Despite the difficulties of building offshore, the area has not escaped the usual number of large new houses, with two or three bathrooms, tall glass walls and sweeping timber decks. I must confess that I, too, hungered for more space in my Tin Shed and extended it until it slotted into my idea of what was necessary. Now I know it's not the size of a house that gives you quality of life. It's community, environment, and learning wisdom from wonder.

When Marty Cowen and her husband, George, bought their weekender on the south-facing shores of Elvina Bay in 1989, the outgoing owners left a two-page document. Not about where to find the fuse box, or the tank switch or anything practical at all. It was about passing on the legacy of the Bays from one generation to the next.

A bush picnic with (from left to right) Dorothy, Hazel and Charles Witt, Gladys and Trix MacPherson and Margaret Witt.

Dear George and Marty,

This is a story of a love affair with the Bays and a quality of life that has lasted for five generations. Yesterday, I was privileged to listen to two gentle ladies share their memories of a lifetime on Pittwater. Their grandfather began the association by staying in a boarding house in Towler's Bay [now the Youth Hostel]. Then their parents, in their courting days, continued by going to house parties at 'Ventnor' and 'Trincomalea' (sic), which at the time belonged to Madame Stephanie, who had a stage built into her lounge and held small theatricals there. Later, the draw of the Bays was such that they purchased their own block and a house was built about 1910.

Now began their own weekends on Pittwater, characterised by epic journeys by coach from Woollahra and then the long row across from Church Point. Ah, but what weekends and holidays they were, and as children were born and grew, they shared with their parents the long rambling walks, the picnics at the lookouts, fishing for leather jacket and whiting and the magnificent oysters from the rocks. These were the days of no electricity; of parties of gay young people dressed in long organdie dresses and creams and dancing to the light of candles and magic lanterns. When their boat was the only one in the bay, and a trip up Pittwater to Broken Bay, could produce the sight of a school of sharks so thick, you could almost walk across them.

The Bays were always a haven, from the gregarious to the recluse. From Tilly Devine who kept a house of ill fame in the City; (but still had time to give parties for orphan children) to Dorothea Mackellar, who wrote 'My Country,' possibly our most loved Australian poem.

Trincomalee *still stands but the once-cleared landscape is now thick with trees.*

These gentle ladies have lived to see a great parade of wonderful characters that have etched their mark on this unique place. They saw the musicale weekends at 'Ventnor' and 'Wyuna' and they even formed a small orchestra with Joan Hammond (who kept her boat [Pankina] in Lovett Bay) to play at charity occasions. They have seen great fires; and the war years, when all boats were confiscated and boatsheds pulled down for fear of Japanese invasion.

In time, another generation was born to spend their summers in the Bay. Long, hot summer holidays, fishing with grandparents, swimming off the beach and oyster cuts from the same rocks; but you still dressed for dinner. Now the fifth generation is here, rambling the same bush paths and sailing across the bay.

Many things have changed, and now there are more of us to share this bit of paradise. Can we fulfil these ladies' fervent hopes? Retain this tranquillity . . . in perpetuity? I believe we can. I believe we must.

May The Pittwater bear each new crop of her sons and daughters just as buoyantly on her shining waters, their sailing boats leaning to the same stiff nor'easters. May there be always; soft wet mornings, with the distant roar of the waterfall and drifts of mist caught in the elbows of the hills. And forever, crisp winter evenings with the smell of wood smoke on the still air, the sound of currawongs on the hill and a flock of white cockatoos flying home.

Each of us while we live here, help to give this place the unique character it has. But without a doubt, however long or short a time we stay, the Bays give us all a precious gift. We are changed somehow, a little larger perhaps for having lived here.

. . . And here's to the next five generations, and our beloved Bays. A legacy.

Love – Cherish – Protect

Jennifer Judson

The Witt family: Charles and Margaret with their children Dorothy, Joyce, Hazel and Kenneth.

Dorothy Witt, one of the much-loved local characters, lived through great fires and the war years.

The 'gentle ladies' were Dorothy Witt and her sister, Hazel Thomson, whose father, Charles, built the house where those generations laughed and played. Now called *Orana*, it was a holiday house until Dorothy, a music teacher who taught piano and never married, and Charles moved there permanently in 1965.

'Despite the transport challenges, my grandfather never gave up going to the opera,' recalled his granddaughter, Prue Sky. 'In those days Lenny Duck was the ferry driver. It was nothing for him to climb back into the ferry at midnight to pick up my aunt and grandfather, who was always dressed in a suit and wearing a hat, when they returned to Church Point.'

Lenny, who was much loved by the community, drove the ferry for more than thirty years. His kindness, compassion, his willingness to do a favour or bend the rules was legendary. He retired after refusing to bow to new regulations demanding he sit for a coxswain's ticket. What would he learn from an exam that three decades of experience hadn't already taught him?

As a child, Prue recalls her mother's tales of holidays and house and tennis parties. Of rowing miles to Clareville for picnics; of long conversations over simple afternoon teas. She remembers the wonder in people's voices as they talked about the birds, the fish, the wallabies; their joy in the physical world.

'I was still expected to wear a skirt to dinner,' Prue says, 'but no-one knew what kind of car you drove. And it didn't matter whether you were a lawyer or a bricklayer; we all communicated with each other because we met on the ferry.'

When she was an adult, Prue and her husband built their home on the block of land next to her grandfather's and raised their children there.

'It was a magical way to live,' she says. 'There was such a sense of community – and security because we all looked out for each other. If your kids disappeared for a while, you never worried about them.'

Charles Witt died in 1971 aged ninety-one. His daughter, Dorothy, or Dorrie as she was known to family (although locally, she was always respectfully referred to as Miss Witt), stayed on until she was eighty-five years old. The house was sold in 1987. Prue and her husband, Greg, left Elvina Bay in 1997 and now have a property near Mudgee in NSW. 'We had a wonderful twenty years of married life there and I have so many memories. Great memories. You know, I still think of the house as "our place". I always will.'

The Witt family picnicking on Pittwater.

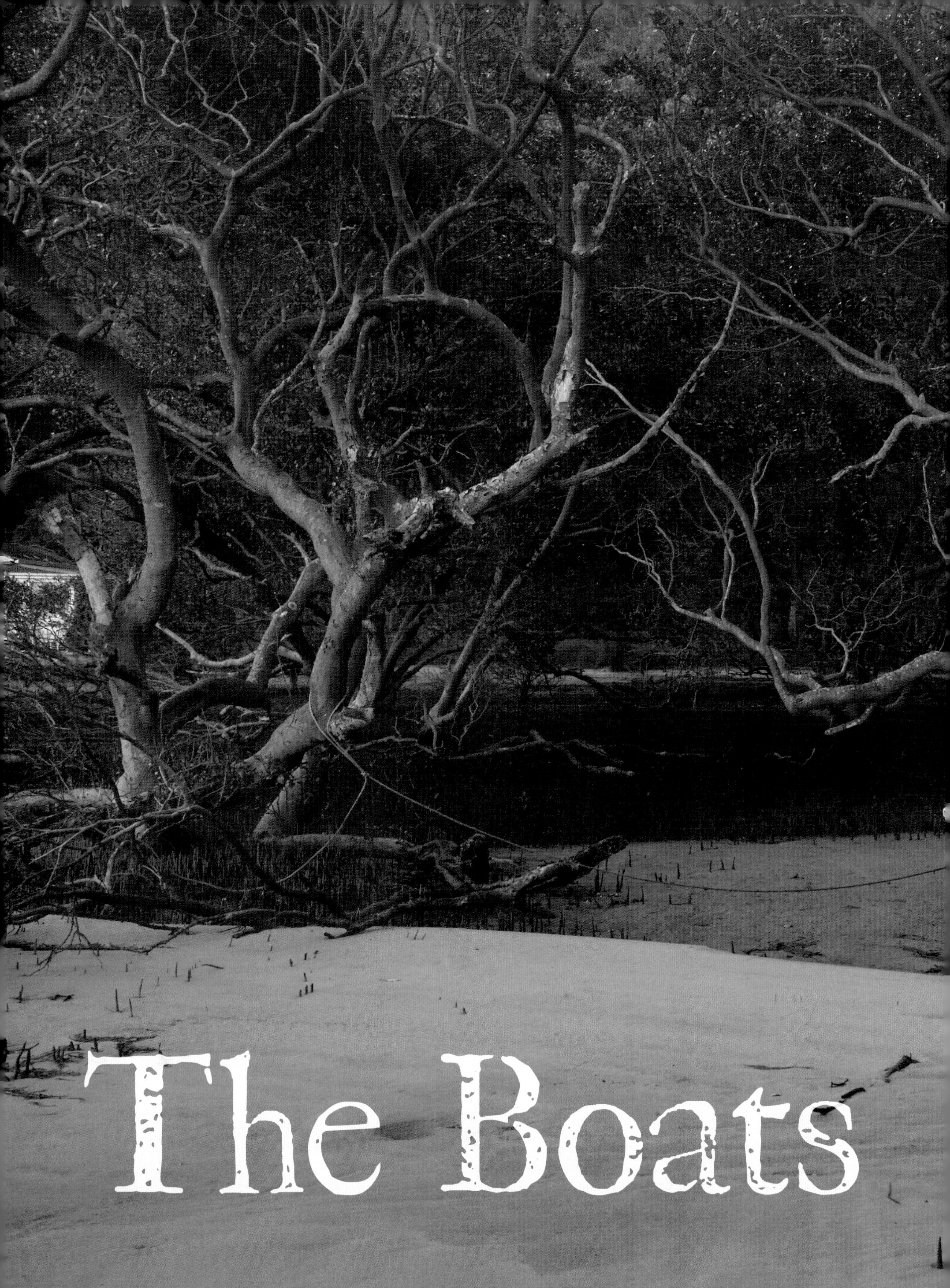

The Boats

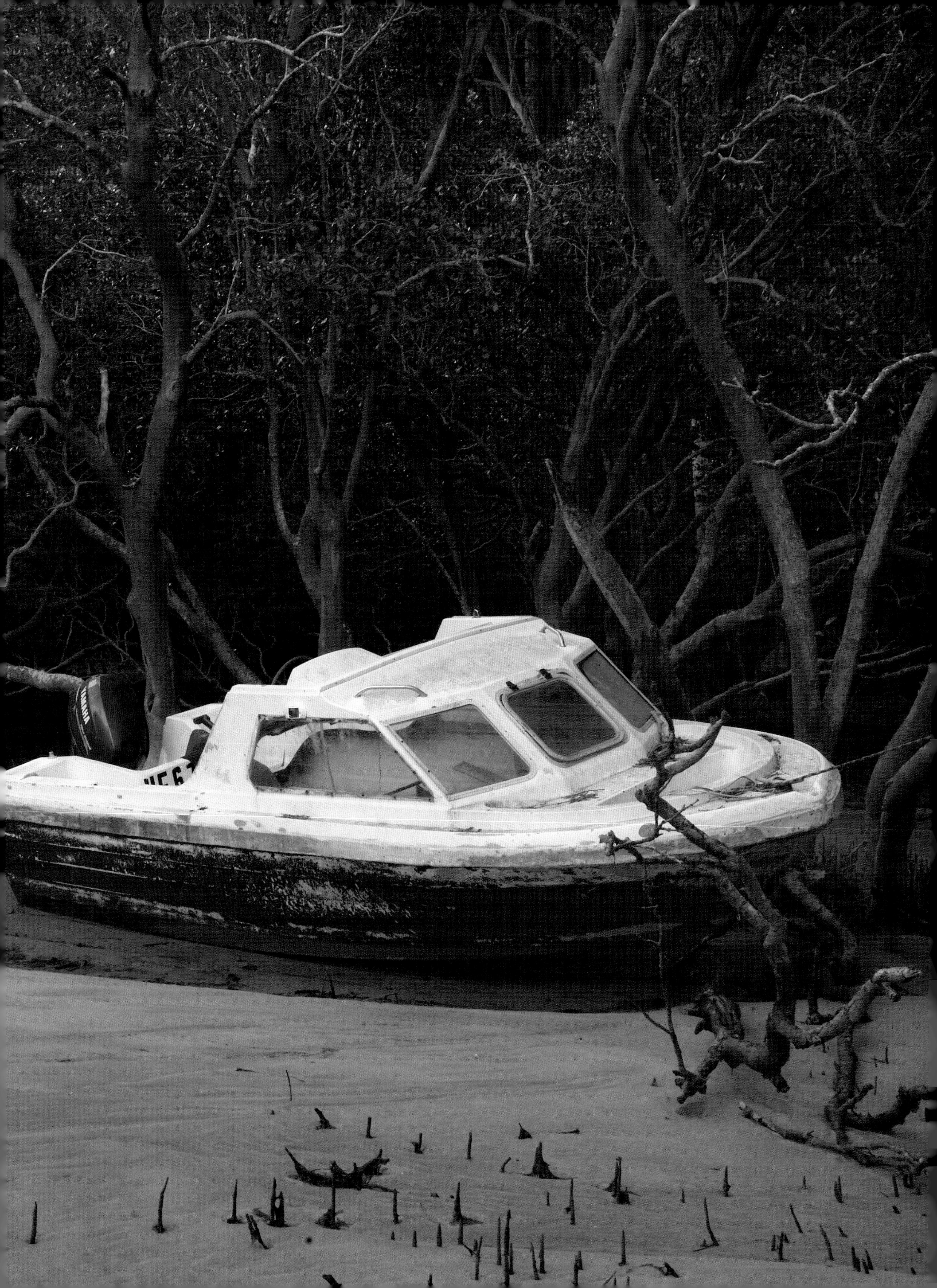
YAMAHA

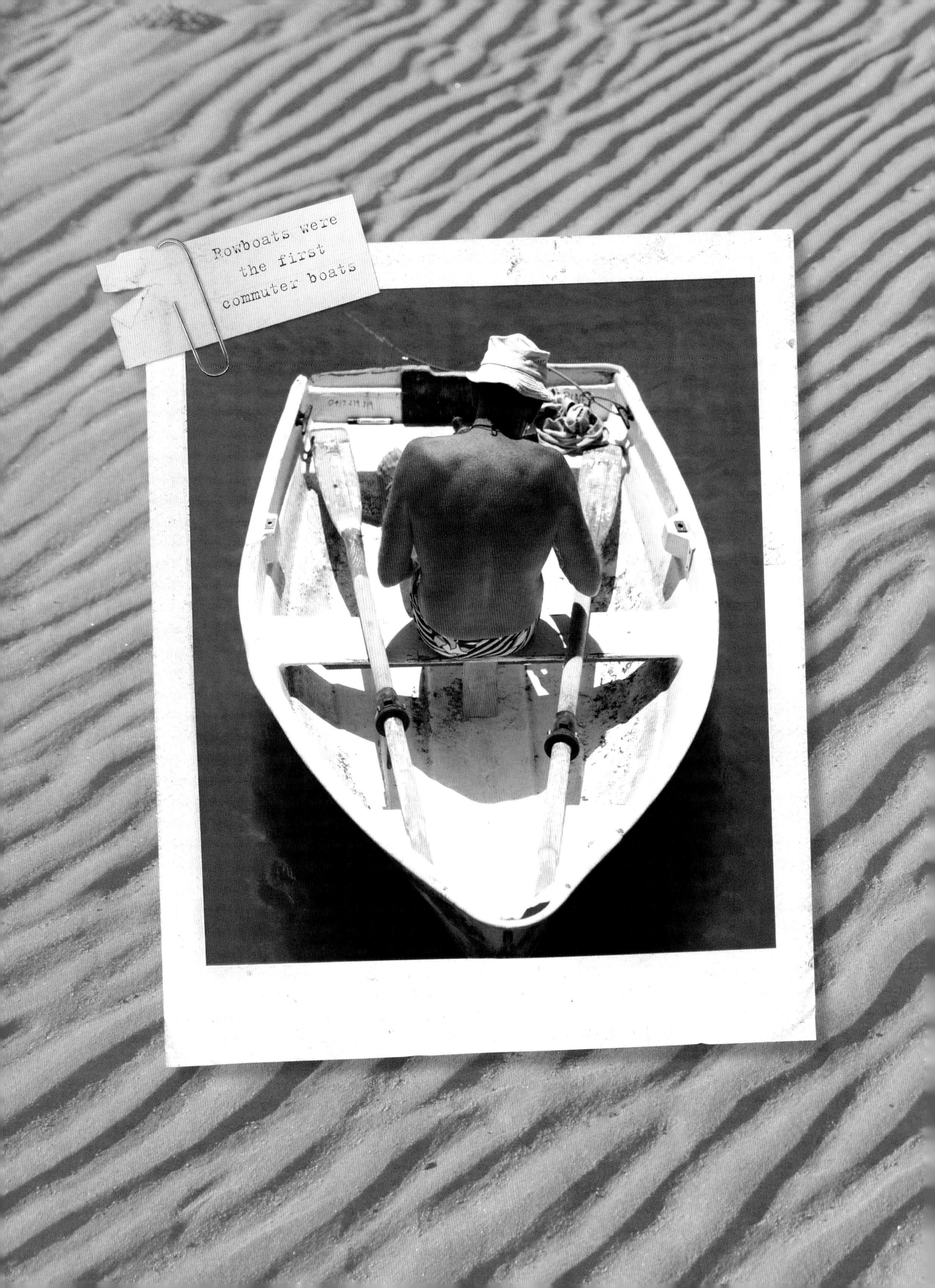
Rowboats were
the first
commuter boats

Slender yachts, banged-up tinnies, cruisers, putt putts and rowboats are a wonderful and energetic parade in the Bays and there's always a friendly wave as you pass by.

I was completely ignorant about boats when I came to Pittwater and hesitated to buy one of my own. I thought I would commute by the local ferry or call on the 24-hour water taxi service if I was in a rush or travelling outside the ferry timetable. Riding the ferry was a great way to meet the locals, exchange information or just feel the stress of the day peel off. The baby-pink water taxis, such a delicate colour for their grunty job, were convenient but expensive if over-used. I soon realised that having my own boat would give me flexibility and freedom.

Nearly everyone on Pittwater has a commuter boat. Either a banged-up tinny, a fibreglass hull or one of the new, very stable plastic boats which come in so many fantastically lurid colours they are known as 'jellybean boats'. There are still rowboats around too, which were the very first commuter boats on Pittwater. They suit anyone who wants to stay fit or who isn't in a hurry and can afford to wait for calm days before setting off. Sometimes I see my neighbour rowing his skiff on a blastingly beautiful, still day. His partner lolls near the bow, a straw hat on her head, her hand trailing in the water. He rows so steadily that to watch him is like meditating. If you wave, he lifts a long skinny leg in greeting so he doesn't break the rhythm.

A box of mangoes, salad greens and the shopping is done for the weekend.

Most boats hang off private jetties at the foot of the garden, others find space at the ferry wharf closest to their homes. To go ashore, boats are tied up at a long, skinny floating public pontoon called Commuter Dock, a short stroll from the car park. If it's a weekday, they can hang three or even four deep, which means jumping – or crawling, depending on your shoes, the chop or the wind – from boat to boat to reach solid ground. It's always wise to choose to tie up close to stable boats.

Stories of falling overboard are so common, unless you sink with your life's savings, all the family photo albums and your mother-in-law, they rarely get told.

To ease gently into a world of gunnels, sterns and bows, rudders, props and tillers, of outboard motors, pull starts and remembering to say dock instead of park, I borrowed a friend's boat to give it a trial go. Nothing about boats resembles driving a car except they are both motor driven. Tillers work in reverse from steering wheels. When you turn off the engine, the boat doesn't stop moving. There are no brakes, clutches or speed indicators. No windscreen wipers to help you see through pouring rain. No headlights to show the way on pitch-black nights. And you are always at the mercy of the wind. It whips seas until you feel the boat might capsize. It hurls waves over the bow. Turns into a chop worse than the corrugations on an outback road. If the engine breaks down, even a light wind can whizz you off course so fast that if you're not quickly rescued, you might find yourself scooting out towards the vast Pacific Ocean. Or more likely, perhaps, crashing up against oyster-encrusted rocks big enough to rip the guts from your hull.

KZ739N
YAMAHA
Quality
Australian
Mangoes

…boats are a way of life.
…any shape, size or colour

A yacht stranded by high tide looks abandoned but when the water comes in it will float serenely once more.

There are no cars in garages, only boats that hang off jetties and pontoons at the bottom of the gardens. Keeping their hulls clean is a must.

WHEN I WAS STILL LIVING ALONE IN THE TIN SHED, Bob told me he was selling one of his two tinnies to design and build a new one. So I decided to take the plunge and make an offer. Barbara insisted part of the package included some driving lessons. We set off, me in the driver's seat, Bob alongside, ready to grab the wheel. I was not an ideal learner. But I didn't understand quite how bad I was until he screamed at me to slow down, his face scrunched up in excruciating pain, his hands cupped around his groin.

'You're . . . breaking . . . my … balls,' he yelled as we hooned over a rutted sea. I pulled back the throttle, aghast. He fell forward so suddenly, he whacked his head hard on the side windscreen.

'Think I need a bit of practice,' I apologised.

A while later, after a few frightening solo forays, I realised being a dumb mug on the water was dangerous. Just like the roads, there are rules. Do you give way to port or starboard? Who has right of way when there's a boat under sail or the ferry is hurtling towards you? How fast can you travel through moorings? What do red and green marker lights indicate? There are many, many more rules that are listed in a little handbook given to you when you apply for a boat licence.

Tinny commuting is pure joy, even in stinging rain. Perhaps because every trip is a physical achievement. Tying and untying, climbing aboard, negotiating swells or rough seas, docking in bad weather. But the water also gives an incredible sense of freedom,

… everyone dreams of restoring
battered old boats to glory and then
sailing away as the sun sets …

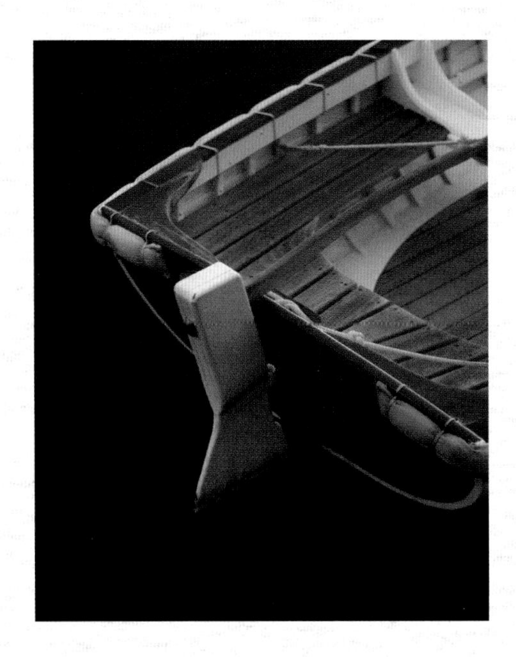

a feeling that if you wanted to, you could keep going and circumnavigate the world in your own time, dropping into exotic tropical islands for coconut juice cocktails, reaching out to touch passing icebergs. Pure fantasy, of course. Half the time, tinnies break down, run out of petrol or spring a leak on the way from your jetty to Church Point.

When neighbours are away, we keep a watchful eye on their boats. If a stern looks low, we race around to check the bilge pump is working or to bail water. Although a storm exploding out of nothing at the end of a scorching day or in the middle of the night can catch us off-guard. That's when most tinnies sink to a watery grave, their engines often knackered for good.

On days when the water is table-smooth, the woody hills threaded with early morning mist, which is the time the kayakers paddle silently around the bay, and you're slowly chugging to The Point because it's too damn beautiful to rush, you don't mind running out of petrol at all. And, anyway, someone always stops to help you.

Once, I was ferrying a friend to The Point when I ran out of fuel at Rocky Point. A neighbour going the other way pulled over to check out the problem.

'Caro's late for the airport,' I told him. 'Can you get her to The Point?'

'Climb aboard!' he said.

Caro gathered her luggage and we held the tinnies together while she swung a leg into his boat. 'Thanks,' she said, smiling at him. He grinned back. A hero.

'I'll give you a tow on the way back,' yelled my neighbour.

Within a few minutes, though, someone else had come to my rescue.

The ferry drivers are unfailingly generous-spirited and set the mood for the day for commuters.

The ferry drivers, from left, Davina, Carrie and Penny, relax at the end of the hectic school run.

THE FERRY SERVICE IS RUN BY PENNY GLEEN, a kind, calm young woman with a beautiful smile, unflagging spirit and a passion for Pittwater. I met her for the first time on a stinking-hot day when she coolly emerged from under the water like a mermaid at our little beach. She'd swum from her home on the other side of Lovett Bay.

'Don't you worry about sharks?' I asked, concerned, because Bob has caught a few metre-long bronze whalers from our pontoon.

She grinned. 'Nah. The sharks around here are all vegetarians.' She and her husband, Simon, a pilot, bought the almost century-old ferry service in February 2008. 'We'd been talking about running our own business for a while but we knew we wouldn't be good in sales and we couldn't think of what else to do.' Penny, an industrial chemist and former logistics manager, had two goals. She didn't want to sit in traffic anymore, and she and Simon, who planned to continue to work as a pilot, also wanted a business that matched their ethics.

'Then we saw a tiny ad in *The Sydney Morning Herald* announcing the ferry service was for sale and it was a case of "why not?" ' she said. 'Providing public transport fulfilled our criteria for being green.'

Within a year, Penny had her coxswain's ticket and a growing knowledge of fuel lines, starter motors, big ends (part of the engine), propeller shafts and the day-to-day idiosyncrasies of their three-strong fleet.

'When I was a kid, I used to joke that when I grew up, I wanted to be a lighthouse keeper or a ferry driver. Be careful what you wish for!' she laughed.

At the end of a summer's day, impromptu parties spring up on the open rear deck as commuters – most of them friends and neighbours – head home, groceries piled around their feet or shoved loosely on the roof of the cabin, a cool drink in hand.

The *Curlew* (originally named *Gloria*) is a 14-metre timber ferry that was built near Wyong on the Central Coast in the 1920s. She is painted navy and white with touches of fire-engine red and slices through the water with matronly efficiency.

The *Amelia K*, an almost-12-metre ferry, is often unkindly referred to as either the 'Tin Can' or the 'Grey Ghost'. She was built in 1996 and named after the daughter of Jack Kirkpatrick, who owned the ferry service at the time. Our timber boat-worshipping community finds little endearing about her clunky metal body and utilitarian lines but she is a good, reliable workhorse. The much smaller timber ferry, *Elvina*, which hangs off a mooring at the mouth of Lovett Bay, is as pretty as a storybook boat, and was built in Palm Beach in the 1920s. She is used if one of the larger ferries is being serviced or is out of action. Often, small groups pack a picnic, a thermos and a bottle of wine and climb on board the *Elvina* for a 45-minute (or longer) charter that sweeps around The Island and the Bays in old-world style.

The ferry drivers are a vital and integral part of the community. Beginning with the first morning run from Bell Wharf to Church Point at 6.20 am, they are the link between the offshore community and the onshore world. They keep an eye on fractious young kids heading to and from school and deliver the mail and newspapers.

… riding the ferry to school
is a way of life when you're an Island or Bays kid …

Australian.
SAFEWAY

The morning and afternoon school run on the old Curlew *is a dream way for kids to commute from Scotland Island and the Bays. There is always time for games or a pretend moment at the helm before the ferry leaves the dock.*

And they offer a hand with the shopping bags, art works, lamps, building materials or equipment, vacuum cleaners and any – sometimes bizarre – bits and pieces that make their way across the water.

Carrie Towers, an island mum, was a deckhand on the chaotic and noisy school run prior to Penny and Simon taking over the business. Now Carrie drives the ferry at the helm in the wheelhouse and brings the vessel alongside the wharf with an expert feather-light touch. Along with shy Rick Peipman, whose six-year-old son, Cooper, is already a fine deckhand, Carrie is now part of the core team of four captains, including Tim Byrne and Michael Ramsay. A few locals, who also have tickets, fill in from time to time, and the 'old masters' – many who have gone on to drive bigger boats – still enjoy returning to do an occasional run. It keeps them in touch with a community they love.

'Can you imagine what it's like to take on a completely new business and have everyone on your side from the beginning?' Penny asked. 'People I've never met before give me a pat and tell me, "You're doing a marvellous job". That goodwill and kindness inspires you. As for the school ferry – well, it's hysterical. Noisy kids everywhere. In summer, they board dripping wet because they've plunged into the water at The Point in their school uniforms. They're full on. Funny. Innocent. Full of subterfuge and honesty at the same time. And wicked. They keep you smiling for the rest of the day.'

THE 24-HOUR WATER-TAXI service runs from a houseboat moored at the mouth of McCarrs Creek and within eyesight of Church Point. When business is slow, and all three taxis are nestled closely, it looks like a mother duck with her ducklings. There's a courtesy phone at The Point that direct dials the service.

Not long after I moved to the Tin Shed, I bought two naughty Jack Russell terrier pups that thought the bush was their personal playground. In the pre-dawn hours, one of them staggered into the bedroom, wheezing so loudly she woke me. I turned on the light, saw her paralysed back legs and realised immediately that she had tick poisoning. Frantic, I called the water taxi. Geoff, a capable and quiet man with a dry sense of humour, arrived in minutes and gently took the puppy out of my arms so I could climb on board.

'The dog will be fine,' he said, passing her back to me like a precious, fragile thing. 'But you'd better calm down or you'll have an accident on the way to the vet.' His words jerked me out of a rising hysteria.

Nothing ever seems to be too much trouble for the drivers. They'll help you to deliver a new dishwasher to your jetty or a case of wine to your door if you are too old or unwell to manage yourself. They'll cheerfully grab and stow twenty pieces of baggage to take on holiday then help you unload at the other end. They'll tow you home if your engine breaks down in the middle of the Bays or give you a friendly pat if they see you are too tired to even speak at the end of a long day. They'll also give you a (still polite) serve if they have to wait a long time at the end of a dock on a busy day while you linger over goodbyes at the end of a boozy lunch or a late party.

Water taxis mean that none of us is ever alone or without help at any time of the day or night. 

Baby-pink water taxis scoot around the Bays all day and night, providing a vital link for the offshore community.

The Bush

When the rains fall steadily in early spring, the bush erupts in waves of pink, gold, blue, yellow and orange and the scent of wildflowers hangs seductively in the air.

It is the dream of glittering bays and waves breaking like soft sighs at the foot of the garden that lures most of us to Pittwater. Sitting for hours at a time, breathing damp sea air scented with oysters, seagrass and mangroves. Watching the water. The same and yet never the same; blue, gold, green, copper, pink, silver and red. The background canvas for night and day, wind and rain, storms with gunfire thunder and jagged lightning, leaping fish, courting sea eagles, a lumbering pelican or two.

In time, I learned to interpret the sounds of the tides. An incoming swallow. An outgoing wheeze. The shadow dance of air darkening the surface of the water. The fizz of a school of baitfish racing ahead of a sharp-toothed predator. But I avoided and felt threatened by the thousands of bristly acres of hostile bush that stretched behind the Tin Shed.

It took a while before I began to explore and finally understand I was living in one of the most diverse and culturally fascinating areas of Sydney. Aboriginal middens rise like tiny temples under sandstone overhangs. Rock carvings of mythical beings from The Dreaming, such as Daramulan – half-man, half-animal – splay in weathered grooves high on the escarpment.

Wildflowers soften the prickly scrub in shades of pink;
delicate and beautiful. Boronia (right).
(clockwise from left) Boronia buds, pink swamp
heath, wax flowers and fringe myrtle.

Wallabies, whales, fish and, I am sure, many more still-undiscovered images are chipped into the landscape. Ancient homage to the Aboriginal creed of the beginning of creation.

Rough fire tracks for emergency vehicles crisscross the Bays although, thankfully, they are mostly used as walking tracks. Locals or tourists who come to stay at the Youth Hostel in Towlers Bay often bring a picnic in a rucksack because there are no coffee shops or restaurants here. What could be more delicious, anyway, than scooping a handful of cool, sweet-tasting water out of any of the creeks that cascade into the bays?

In the early morning or so late in the afternoon it is almost dusk, rusty-chested swamp wallabies stand and stare intently and bounce off in sudden flight only if you pass too closely. In seasons when the rain falls steadily and the bush unfolds in layers of green, cheeky joeys peek from pouches or stand hesitantly alongside their mothers until they grow in size and courage. At first they beguile. Then I tried to grow a garden. And it was war.

At night, they thumped and rampaged, stripping new growth from tender young plants until they withered and died. They reached up to grab the boughs of my lemon trees and dragged them down until they fractured. They snapped off flower heads before they had a chance to bloom. My small vegetable patch became their personal salad bowl until nothing survived. I ranted and raved. Then stopped. I lived in the bush. I had to adjust. To twist it to my will would be to lose its integrity. Where would shy lyrebirds with their stolen songs hide? Or clumsy brush turkeys build their nesting mounds? Where would wild orchids, pink and delicate, or tiny vanilla lillies with their fragile mauve throats, grow? Would the leopard moths that salsa through the bush survive? And the black cockatoos with red sirens under their tails – what would happen to them if the casuarinas disappeared and there were no nuts for them to feed on? How easy it is to chip away without noticing what gets lost – until one day there is nothing left.

Of all the walks – and there are many – in what I eventually came to understand was a truly wondrous backyard, Flagstaff is my favourite. It begins a little way beyond the Lovett Bay ferry wharf, where there's a thorny tunnel through a copse of baby cabbage palms. No wider than a wallaby's track, after high winds or raging storms it is often strewn

... at night the **bush** comes alive ...
sugar gliders, possums, wallabies, owls
and **bandicoots** ...

with fallen trees. It crosses a creek with a tiny waterfall in wet weather, then razorbacks up a steep hillside to a rocky outcrop at the summit. From here you can see Lovett Bay, Scotland Island and the crammed armadas of yachts at Newport – so distant they look like flocks of seagulls resting on the water. Beyond lies the pale blue line of the Pacific Ocean.

It is called Flagstaff because it is the highest point in the area and someone, at some time, hammered a socket for a flagpole and strong steel hooks to tie guy ropes into the rocks. There is a timber seat there, too, which Bob repairs from time to time. During the days of Eccleston du Faur's grand plans, sandstone steps, which still remain, were set into the steepest parts of the pathway. A cool cave just a few feet from the top became a welcome shady shelter for walkers to boil a billy and eat their sandwiches or cake. The bush, as dense as it seems to be when you battle through it, is more bony than shady.

When we are lucky enough to have a wet spring, the landscape erupts. Banksia trees alight with flower cones like golden candles. Xanthorrhoeas sprout long, sap-laden spears from their grassy skirts. Mauve grevillea flowers curl in spidery fists. Pink-skinned apple gums (*angophora costata*) fizz with creamy flowers and wattles (*acacias*) create clouds of honeyed perfume so strong it makes you dizzy. Wildflowers are prolific. Boronia, wax flowers, flannel flowers, dianella, hardenbergia, ti-tree and many, many more, some so tiny only an expert eye picks them out.

Rusty-chested swamp wallabies lurk shyly in the bush.

The picnic cave at Flagstaff where billies were boiled in the old days. Flowers such as mountain devil and banksia grew in abundance.

Sometimes, as I make my way back down to the shore, I remember being told that there are more plant species between Sydney and Newcastle than in the whole of Europe. And I send a silent thank-you to Eccleston du Faur.

The bush is constantly under threat from invasive plant species. The dreaded lantana, asparagus fern, crofton weed, bamboo, mother-of-millions, and many more. Without the effort and diligence of members of the bush regeneration groups, infestations would threaten the plant diversity of the area.

Volunteers meet on designated Saturdays, Sundays or Mondays, leather tool bags slung around their hips, ready to attack one small area at a time. (Clearing large areas can create even bigger problems, providing spaces for weeds to take hold again.) Huge white bags, supplied by the council, are filled with weeds, then left alongside the fire trails to be collected and disposed of by the National Parks.

Joining a bush regeneration group is a great way to enter into community life on Pittwater. You meet the neighbours, learn about good and bad plants, and the species – if there are any – that wallabies leave alone. Although experience suggests that while wallabies may not eat grevilleas at one house they will devour them at another. The work is as hard or as easy as you can manage and the simple act of spending slow time in the bush opens your eyes to its magic. It is an easy and pleasant way to learn the names of local plants, their seasons and their perfumes, and to see the damage that happens if noxious weeds are allowed to run wild.

It is work of passion and commitment, undertaken by people who do not want to hear their children or grandchildren asking: 'Why didn't you do something about it before it was too late?'

There is a salt marsh at the end of Towlers Bay, lush with mangroves and reeds. A freshwater creek runs into the tidal flats. Without many of us noticing it, buffalo grass crept to the edges of the reeds and grew so thickly it formed a bank. The tide isn't always high enough to flood over it to replenish the marsh. I think of the marsh whenever I feel tempted to succumb to laziness and selective blindness as I pass a cluster of crofton weed. Who could guess that a single rogue runner of buffalo grass could, in time, silently change the landscape? And what about the bamboo? Planted for a quick privacy screen or an Asian look, some types are rampant from the moment the first root sinks into the ground and thunders into the bush like a conquering army. It takes two bush 'regen' volunteers to stop the spread – one to cut the cane, the other to paste on poison within ten seconds of cutting. Even then, it only slows growth and each plant has to be dug out, roots and all, one by one.

BUSH

…each invasive plant has to be **dug out**, **roots and all**, one by one…

Typically, on Pittwater, bush regeneration turns into a social get-together. Especially on Asparagus Fern Out Day. That's when Penny gives free ferry transport to onshore weeders who come to help for the day, and the locals provide a picnic lunch. Mostly, though, the work is done by neighbours, their backsides flat on the ground in the middle of bushland, quietly attacking a small patch of weeds; a white bag alongside, gently easing plants out of the ground so that not a single root is broken and left to regrow.

It doesn't take long to develop an eye for foreign invaders. On morning walks we'll stop to pull out a lantana seedling that's suddenly struck. Or dive off the track to ease out a new pocket of crofton weed. Once, my neighbour and I stood in front of a vine neither of us recognised. She pinched a leaf to identify it from her botanical books. It was morning glory – a plant that's so tough and invasive it threatens bushland from one end of Australia to the other. We dug it out the next day.

Someone (nearly always Ann and Nick from Little Lovett Bay, who do a couple of hours work very early in the morning) has begun to eradicate, limb by limb, one of the strong lantana infestations in the Bays. When the thick growth has been whittled to the ground, they carefully excavate around the roots until they can be removed without even a tear. Within weeks the native bush erupts to reclaim its territory.

The Barges

9
60

Early in the morning the working barges begin their day, timing their schedules with the tides and chugging through the Bays with their heavy loads.

The water, a deeper blue than the sky in the heat of summer, is a highway for yachts, launches, speed boats, commuter tinnies, and the services that keep offshore life running smoothly. Garbage-collection barges, pile-driving barges, barges that deliver building or landscaping materials and barges, too, for shipping your furniture in and out.

In small communities such as ours, there is always a natural curiosity about newcomers. Will they fit in? Will they love, cherish and protect? Are they weekenders or here to stay? Although we are quick to welcome, people are not immediately embraced. In communities, you earn your place over time and takers are quickly sussed out. We watch closely for a while . . . as I was watched when I first came here. I'd let my wildly exuberant Jack Russell terriers run wild. They acted as though they'd been let loose in their own private game reserve and I saw no harm until Bob and Barbara quietly took me aside. 'The puppies will grow and they will hunt,' they explained. 'You must keep them under control.'

Now that I know and understand so much more, I, too, gently suggest what's acceptable behaviour or what will incite ire. It's personal choice whether to respond or ignore local advice. I have only heard of one case, decades ago, when a man so affronted local values, community pressure forced him to leave.

High tide, a sunny sky and a bunch of cheery blokes take the anguish out of moving day.

RUSS IS A QUIETLY spoken bloke with a tranquil black and white border collie called Max. The two of them cruise the Bays like master and commander, although it's hard to tell which is which. Max stretches out on the barge with the cattle-crossing warning sign like he's a canine god. Russ pushes from behind in a tiny tinny with an outboard motor.

Russ is the local removalist. He transports fridges, sofas, washing machines, tables, boxes, armchairs and pot plants. Even, bizarrely, a zebra and a giraffe (live ones hired for children's birthday parties at nearby Palm Beach).

'It's all about balance,' Russ says, as though it's no big deal. 'You learn to judge the wakes from passing boats and adjust your angle to suit.'

Household goods are piled high without even a cord to tie them tight, until you feel that surely, they must topple overboard.

Russ tries to organise his schedule to coincide with high tide so the truck and the boat are level at Cargo Wharf. At low tide, there's a deep drop from land to water and the job is much harder. It takes perfect balance, brute strength and an understanding of the movement of the water to make it all work successfully.

There are apocryphal stories about moving days, some so old and retold so often they have become lore. I have heard of a woman who shipped all her worldly goods into her new home on Scotland Island and within two hours, decided it was a dreadful mistake.

PALFINGER
18155

YAMAHA

…it takes perfect balance, brute strength and an instinctive understanding of the movement of the water to move possessions in and out of homes without losing even a broom to the watery depths…

… garbage pick-up day as the truck
cruises the Bays on a barge nudged along by a tug …

She left immediately and never returned. I have heard that once long, long ago an entire cargo of household goods went overboard never to be retrieved. I even heard of one removalist who liked to arrange a sofa, a pot plant, a coffee table and a cool drink on the bow of the barge. Then he'd invite the owners aboard so they could ride to their new home in Pittwater-style comfort.

TOBY JAY AND DAVE SHIRLEY own a beautiful, elegant, 40-foot scow called the *Laurel Mae.* Designed and built in 1990 by local shipwright Mick Cardiff and his partner, Graham Botham (who died in 2007), she is a jewel. Made from the carefully hewn timber of grey iron-barks and spotted gums, the towering eucalypts indigenous to this part of Pittwater, she and the skippers hold the firm affection of the community. On Clean-Up Australia Day, volunteers clamber aboard to glide from bay to bay, ferry wharf to ferry wharf, gathering unclaimed (or unacknowledged) junk. Old tinnies. Discarded building material. Timber pallets. Ruptured kayaks. Dead stoves. The ugly and untidy clutter that accumulates when the effort and organisation of removing it to the tip is fraught with expense and difficulty.

We bring picnic baskets, thermoses of coffee and ice-boxes filled with beer and wine. At the end of the day, the barge ties up at the Lovett Bay boatshed and if there's not a total fire ban, Toby barbecues sausages on an open fire in the hollow of two boulders for his helpers before he returns to his mooring off The Island.

Picnics &

Cooks

Lovett Bay picnic, 2009

Picnics – at the water's edge, high on the escarpments, in a quiet sandy corner or even in a rowboat bobbing on the water – are a way of life and bring people together for fun, to raise money or mark a special event.

Living with a bay at the foot of the garden felt like being on permanent holiday. This is the stuff of dreams, I thought, when I first found my Tin Shed. I still feel the same way. In the winter, we watch the sun sink behind the hills, turning the trees high on the escarpment into lacy silhouettes. In the final moments of daylight, the water glistens darkly like black marble. Still. Mysterious. Achingly beautiful. Frigid air races down the escarpment to unfurl like a heavy blanket on the bay.

When the weather warms a little and the fish come back, it is lovely to light a fire at the edge of the shore in an old washing machine drum set on a few bricks.

It became a habit to invite friends from other bays. They chugged into the mouth of Lovett Bay with engine noises that became so familiar I could tell, without looking, who was about to arrive. Caro and David's hollow cough. Nick and Ann's high-pitched grunt. Stewart and Fleury's growl. Each with a dish in hand until our little picnic turned into a feast.

It is always oddly quiet around the campfire. Perhaps the beauty of a rising yellow moon, or ghostly mangroves hovering on the far shore, make words inadequate. Voices stay muted

until a story, well told, sets off deep laughter. Which sparks another story until we all kick in with a tale of our own. There is such pleasure in the gentle stories of community.

Sometimes we take our fishing rods and throw lines into the bay. If we're lucky and catch a bream or flathead, it is quickly cleaned on the pontoon and thrown in a pan of sizzling butter. We each fork a bite until there is none left and the head and carcass is then used to bait crab pots.

Picnics are the soul of community get-togethers.

Whenever there's any event, it takes only a moment or two to pack a basket full of delicious goodies to take along on an adventure.

The joy of picnics, though, is not only the food, which is rarely fancy unless it's a special occasion – just a couple of sandwiches, a piece of fruit and a bottle of water for a walk through the national park. If there are two of you to share the load, perhaps cake and a thermos of coffee as well. For the boat, perhaps fresh prawns or a cooked chicken – finger food, so there's no washing up.

The pleasure, really, comes from pushing yourself physically. Walking or sailing, then stopping to rest on a rock, or throwing out the anchor. Hot. Sweaty. Breathless.

When you are still, there's time to carefully look at what's around you; to notice colours and textures you've never seen before. The vastness of Pittwater and Ku-ring-gai reinforces the smallness of each of us.

Everyone brings a dish of something delicious to turn a simple picnic into a feast.

Setting up is half the fun and everyone helps carry tables, chairs, crockery and cutlery. If a sudden squall rolls in briefly, we shelter in the Lovett Bay boatshed until it passes.

How rare and extraordinary it is to have this kind of wildness on the edge of Australia's largest city. And it is wild! I will never forget the day I heard strange, scratchy but heavy-footed steps in the hallway. I turned just in time to see a five-foot-long goanna rush past me into the study, so close I could smell his rancid breath. He climbed onto the day bed and flung himself at a closed window. I screamed and jumped up from the computer where I was working, grabbed my still (unbelievably!) sleeping dog from under the desk and ran down the hallway yelling for Bob.

'Didn't you hear me screaming?' I asked when he finally sauntered in from the chook shed.

'Yeah, but you stopped.'

'It usually goes silent when you're dead. Or something,' I grumped.

'Too late to make a difference then,' he said, grinning and picking up a broom to chase the goanna back into the bush.

...kids, low tide and a golden sunset at a Lovett Bay picnic...

Kids run themselves ragged in the bush, and neighbours gather regularly at the fire shed fundraisers.

The Cooks & Bay Recipes

Nearly everyone living offshore is a good cook. For two main reasons. The first and probably most important is that there aren't any restaurants that will deliver takeaway across the water. If you don't cook, you don't eat. The second is that once you plunge through the front door at the end of a long day, there's no way you want to desert the peace and beauty of home for noisy crowds and grimy pavements. And anyway, what could be better than a simple meal made from good ingredients, eaten at a table on a deck, watching yachts under sail race in the twilight series? Or listening to a cheeky penguin quacking and diving in the bay. Or watching the sun set or a moon rise. Even the swankiest five-star establishments cannot match it.

Like country people, our isolation forces us to be creative, adventurous and adept at conjuring delicious food out of pantry and freezer staples. We cannot dash around the corner to the butcher or supermarket if we all suddenly decide to have a neighbourhood barbecue – not without losing our parking space in the car park, anyway, and that's unthinkable.

WEST PITTWATER BUSH FIR
ELVINA BAY

Some cooks, though, are not just good, they're spectacular. Such as Tim from Towlers Bay, Lisa from Elvina Bay and Cher from Scotland Island. There are many more, of course, with specialties that range from Persian omelettes to whole roast pig, from hot and spicy curries to sublime middle-Eastern vegetarian dishes. But these three are long-standing stalwarts at fundraisers and community events. They may be self-taught but they can whip up an exotic menu for more than one hundred people, stay within a tight budget and make it all look deceptively easy.

The most regular cook-a-thon is the once-a-month fundraiser for the Elvina Bay fire shed. Lisa and her husband, Roy, an electrician, who is also chief of the Elvina Bay Volunteer Fire Brigade, are the guiding forces behind the hugely popular dinners. Over the years Lisa's cooking has become so legendary that when a back-burn is organised to thin vegetation before the bushfire season, Elvina Bay never has any trouble finding helpers. They line up for her wicked chocolate brownies and moist sour cream cakes; for her baguettes filled with chicken, roasted capsicum and rocket; or rare roast beef with bitey tamarind chutney, cucumber and lettuce; or char-grilled vegetables with a homemade pesto.

On the first Saturday of each month (although sometimes the dinners are suspended during winter) people drift towards the fire shed from about six o'clock onwards. Kids swing

on ropes hanging from trees. If the tide is out, they bolt through the mud flats until they flake (rarely) or get called to dinner. Then they rush up to the fire shed kitchen table, worn out, happy, dirty and barefoot despite the rough ground, to pounce on whatever the chef du jour has prepared for them. Everyone lends a hand to set up trestle tables, folding chairs and coloured lights until the waterfront looks like a seaside restaurant in a small village on the Mediterranean. The bay turns black, the sky glitters with stars and the casuarinas begin to sing in a light breeze. Food is served by whoever is closest, everyone takes a turn washing up the mismatched plates and cutlery, and the low mumble of the community hums along with the night bush song.

The annual AGM for the local Woody Point Yacht Club, which is named after a scrubby finger of land covered with spindly, ill-nourished spotted gums on the southern side of Towlers Bay, also depends on volunteers to cook the dinner. Traditionally held at the Lovett Bay boatshed, there have been many chefs and many memorable meals, but the time Tim grilled lamb cutlets with a lemon, thyme, butter and olive sauce and served it with fried polenta and a salad of bitter greens was one of the best. Cher, who once owned the Caotic Chook chicken shop in Mona Vale, is famous for her harissa and golden roasted lemon and rosemary spatchcocks; her garlic, white balsamic and rosemary quail

A safely contained fire in an old washing machine drum is an autumn and spring picnic tradition.

legs and her heady coq au vin. Her butter chicken is a smooth symphony of spices and she can put a cheese plate together so that it looks like a work of art. For a while, she and Lisa put on dinners at the Scotland Island Community Hall, cooking amazing dishes in a very basic kitchen. Together, they have cooked to raise money for the local preschool, high school, for kids needing money to compete overseas, for anyone suddenly in need of a few extra dollars.

They are people with big hearts and generous spirits – people who work hard but are always prepared to work even harder for a good cause.

Any person or group who wants to, has a chance to be a chef for the day at the Elvina Bay fire shed. Food is generally prepared and cooked at home, then lugged to a tinny to be transported across the water. There is an efficient old oven in the shed but it's not big enough to cater for around one hundred people.

The Elvina Bay Book Club women recently decided to host a Greek night for the first dinner of 2009. Moussaka, we all happily agreed, until someone mentioned it was going to be 42 degrees on the day and we all wilted at the prospect of browning 30 kilos of lamb mince. 'Lamb shoulders,' we decided, 'slow roasted so there's no fiddling around with grilling eggplant and making gallons of béchamel sauce.' Unfortunately, the price of lamb had just escalated due to extended heatwaves in the country. A quick internet search revealed Greeks also ate pork. Marilyn, it turned out, had a particularly delicious recipe for pork shoulders, and called the local supermarket to get a deal on the meat.

Joy took on the hefty job of buying tomatoes, cucumbers, red onions, fetta, olives, watermelon and all the ingredients for a delicious bean cassoulet.

Meanwhile, Michelle volunteered to make vegetarian moussaka; Lisa said she'd cook baklava for dessert; Margie, a woman who is both creative and efficient, borrowed CDs of Greek music from the library; Jackie brought old jam jars to put tea light candles in; and we ransacked our cupboards to find gingham tablecloths. Jackie volunteered to make chicken souvlaki for the kids, and Judy and Marilyn said they'd do the shopping for the ingredients for the pork dish. We divided ten large shoulders to cook between us, and the feast was on!

I must confess, I undercooked my pork shoulders to the point that they were inedible. Everyone laughed and said, 'We'll recook them on Monday for the fireys' meeting.'

Food galore at the Woody Point AGM in the Lovett Bay boatshed.

Throughout the day as temperatures soared, smoke filled the sky from bushfires north and south of us, hazing the landscape like sooty grey fur. The smell of burning bush made us edgy even though the sea breeze was in and predicted to get stronger in the early afternoon. It would force back any flames that might try to rampage towards us. But it was a reminder that although our fire shed dinners are great community fun, the underlying reason for them is to raise money so that when fires hit, we have the right equipment to fight hard, efficiently, effectively and as safely as possible.

Later that night, as the last tables and chairs were packed away, Brigitte's dinner ticket sales were notched at one hundred and nine. A good turnout.

The next morning Australia woke to news of death and destruction in Victoria's worst bushfires in history. They seem to have become a part of life in these times of record heat and endless dry. We listened to the radio and heard stories of tragedy and heroism. Then fell silent as the death toll rose to horrific numbers.

When the final costs of the dinner were tallied, we'd raised $2500 on the night. It was donated to the bushfire fund in Victoria. Food brings us together in celebration or crisis. It sustains, is understood, appreciated and even – occasionally – applauded.

BAY RECIPES

Lisa's chocolate chip biscuits

125 g unsalted butter, softened
1¼ cups packed brown sugar
1 tsp vanilla essence
1 egg, lightly beaten
1½ cups plain flour
½ tsp baking powder
pinch of salt
250 g block of dairy milk chocolate, roughly chopped

Preheat oven to 180°C. Cream butter and sugar until light. Add vanilla and egg and beat to combine. Stir in sifted flour, baking powder and salt until just combined. Gently stir through chocolate pieces. Spoon cooking mixture onto greased and lined trays to allow for spreading. Cook 15–20 minutes until they turn pale gold.

Ann's secret garden marmalade

3 seville oranges for bitterness, or 3 sweet oranges
1 kg cumquats
1½ kg sugar
2 litres of water

Wash the fruit. Simmer the whole oranges for an hour. Half an hour before the end, add whole cumquats. Allow fruit to cool. Remove fruit and chop, reserving pips, and return fruit to water. Boil pips separately in a very small amount of water (or you can tie pips in a muslin cloth) for a few minutes. Strain water into the general fruit mix (or add parcel of pips). Boil rapidly for 15 minutes, then add sugar and boil until mixture sets – about 40 minutes.

When my mother was old, she found chopping the fruit quite difficult so she softened it first using this method,' Ann said.

Lisa and her choc chip bikkies.

Chicken and seafood paella

Extra virgin olive oil for cooking
1½ Spanish onions, finely chopped
5 cloves of garlic, finely chopped
½ tsp sea salt, to taste
freshly ground black pepper
½ tsp chilli flakes
saffron powder
18 green prawns, shelled, deveined, tails on
2 chorizo sausages, diced large
100 g smoked bacon, lardons
2 tomatoes, peeled and chopped
1 yellow pepper, deseeded and chopped
1 red pepper, deseeded and chopped
½ tsp 'La Chinata' smoked paprika
5 tsp chopped flat leaf parsley
2 tsp tomato paste
375 g 'Calasparra' paella rice
1 litre fresh chicken stock
1 lemon, cut into wedges

Heat a paella pan with a splash of olive oil. Add the finely chopped onion, garlic and chicken and cook gently for a couple of minutes to seal the chicken. Add peppers, tomatoes, bacon and sausage and cook for a further few minutes. Add chilli flakes, paprika, saffron, half the parsley and tomato paste, then add in the rice and chicken stock all at the same time. Season.

Stir through and leave for 20 minutes, on a simmer, to absorb. Give the pan a gentle shake every five minutes but do not stir the rice. Lastly, add the prawns and cook through. Turn off heat and let rest for five minutes to allow the rice to absorb the last of the moisture.

Add extra parsley to pan and place in centre of table 'share style' and add wedges of lemon. Serve with aioli. Serves six.

This is Mark Holland's (from Food Stuff in Mona Vale) famous Northern Beaches paella. It can be increased to cater for 150 people if you have a big enough pan.

Tim's lamb backstraps

4 lamb backstraps
2 tsp cumin seeds
zest of one lemon
olive oil

SAUCE
Greek yoghurt
crushed garlic
chopped coriander leaves

SALAD
mixed greens, red capsicum
cooked chickpeas
olive oil
lemon juice

1 cup cooked couscous

Rub lamb with cumin seeds, lemon rind and salt. Allow to sit for a few minutes. Heat olive oil in a frying pan and sear meat on both sides for 2–3 minutes. Remove from pan and allow to rest for five minutes. The lamb should be pink when sliced.

Stir Greek yoghurt, crushed garlic and chopped coriander leaves together. Allow enough time for the flavours to combine. Season to taste.

Toss salad ingredients in a very small amount of olive oil and squeeze over lemon juice, season with salt and pepper.

To serve, slice lamb and arrange on a bed of couscous. Add yoghurt mixture on the side and pour a little more over the salad.

Brandy cream for Christmas pudding

1 egg, separated
½ cup of icing sugar
1 cup cream
2 tbs (or more) brandy

Beat egg white until stiff. Gradually add 1/4 cup of icing sugar. Fold in lightly whisked egg yolk. In a separate bowl, whip cream until stiff. Add 1/4 cup of icing sugar. Fold in as much brandy as you like but a minimum of two tablespoons. Fold the two mixtures together.

This came off a tag on a Christmas pudding made by Lyn Reid from Monroe West Station, via Deniliquin, NSW. In Lovett Bay, Andrew and Matt make a wish as they stir the pudding.

Jeanne's lemon thins

260 g plain flour
250 g unsalted butter
180 g caster sugar
1 large fresh egg
1 tsp vanilla essence
zest of 1 lemon
1 tsp salt

Whizz sugar with the zest in a food processor. Add butter and whizz until combined. Add egg and vanilla essence. Add salt and flour until just combined – a really quick whizz.

Divide dough in half, roll into a 4 cm log and wrap in plastic cling wrap. Refrigerate at least two hours.

Heat oven to 180°C. Cut logs into 1 cm thick slices and bake on a baking sheet for 10–12 minutes or until golden brown. Cool on a wire rack.

These are wonderful biscuits to serve warm from the oven. Keep the mixture frozen in rolls, and cut and cook when friends arrive for a cuppa.

Cher's rosy spatchcocks

4 spatchcocks
10 garlic cloves, peeled and crushed
bunch of fresh rosemary, leaves removed
from stems and crushed
½ cup white balsamic vinegar
1 tbs lemon juice
½ cup olive oil
salt and pepper

Halve spatchcocks, cutting out the thick ridge of backbone.

Whisk olive oil, lemon juice and vinegar together until thick and creamy. Add other ingredients, whisk. Put poultry in shallow dish, pour over marinade. Place in the fridge and marinate overnight, turning occasionally.

Preheat oven to 200°C. Transfer spatchcock halves to baking dish and cook uncovered for 25–30 minutes, skin side up, until golden and cooked through. Or barbecue with lid closed, cooking bone side to the flames.

Yachts &

Putt Putts

Yachts under billowing white sails glide splendidly along the water as the summer twilight races begin, with the joyful company, occasionally, of dolphins and penguins.

Summer officially begins when we turn our clocks ahead an hour for daylight saving. Unofficially, it starts two weeks earlier when long, short, fat, slim, young and sleek or old and cosy yachts line up at the Lovett Bay Boatshed to have their bottoms scraped and anti-fouled in preparation for the first Woody Point Yacht Club twilight sail of the season.

The creation of this quirky, disorganised little yacht club, where anything that floats can race, is a typical Pittwater story. In the early 1980s, a gorgeous, larrikin bloke called Tim Shaw rented a boatshed belonging to the closest house to Woody Point. Tim and one of his old school mates, Clint, shared the space and lived idyllically. Another school mate, David, had a bed there whenever he wanted it. Fishing from their deck, swimming in tepid water on sizzling days, and hosting parties with such joyful gusto and spontaneity they became wonderfully notorious.

Sailing the twilight races during the summer season of the Woody Point Yacht Club with the official start boat, Percerverance.

Tim owned an old 18-foot putt putt called *Pelican*, with a single cylinder Blaxland motor and a beautifully voluptuous shape. She'd been abandoned and left to rot so Tim decided to restore her. While he was agonising over a scarf joint and a couple of bits of timber with the boys, they discussed the exquisite lines of the *Black Swan* – the tender vessel for the New York Yacht Club. It was 1983, and just a couple of weeks after Alan Bond had won the America's Cup for Australia.

'As a joke,' said David, 'we decided we should write to the NYYC and offer them reciprocal rights for the use of *Pelican* (still unseaworthy) in return for our use of the magnificent *Black Swan* should we ever visit New York.

'To appear bona fide, we realised we needed to become an entity and clearly, since it was all about boats, we thought we should call ourselves a yacht club.'

At the time, they were standing on Woody Point. Hence Woody Point Yacht Club. David, an industrial engineer, sculptor and artist, designed a letterhead and a cloth badge, limited to an edition of one hundred. The badge was sold to a few, select locals within the boating fraternity, to recoup costs. The letterhead was never printed in any quantity because only one was ever required.

'We never did receive a reply from the NYYC,' David mused. (Although their offer must have been filed somewhere in the hallowed archives of the club. A few years later, a letter arrived addressed to the Commodore of the Woody Point Yacht Club, inviting him to tender for the rights to hold the America's Cup! It was read out at the Annual General Meeting amidst much hilarity.)

…the primary **motivation**

of the Woody Point Yacht Club is the enjoyment

of Pittwater and its **inhabitants**…

Pelican was eventually restored with the help of locals. 'A few of us decided to give Tim a hand every Sunday morning through the summer,' according to Philip, a Scotland Island resident. 'We'd all bring a bottle of champagne and something to throw on the barbecue. Then we'd do a bit of sanding or whatever and when we'd finished work – or to be truthful, often before we'd begun – we'd pop the cork.'

By the mid-1980s, the regular gathering of this rowdy, irreverent group of timber-boat-loving non-conformists with one thing in common (only one of them owned a yacht) became known as the Woody Point Yacht Club. By then, a membership fee of two dollars was introduced to cover costs. And every Sunday, the meeting was declared by opening the first bottle of booze while Tim fired up the hotplate.

Beetle, one of the founding members, recalled: 'Occasionally, the neighbour's wife would send her husband, Barry, to the boatshed to tell us to quieten down. But Barry loved a party and he joined in. In appreciation, the boys voted him the first commodore of their fledgling yacht club, and he is the first and only patron.'

Inevitably, many meetings turned into parties that continued late into the night. To cater for the growing crowds, Tim, an engineer, built a spit big enough to roast a pig, a lamb and several chickens simultaneously.

Finally *Pelican* was launched. 'During a weekend barbecue not long after, there was some friendly banter about putt putts. The challenge went out for a race around Scotland Island. That's when the seed was planted for a more formal event.'

As the membership grew, more and more timber boats were being lovingly restored by local boaties who'd find them washed up on the shore or left to rot in slipways. Soon, there were twenty-eight boats competing for a perpetual trophy made from an old exhaust water mixer. And that's how the Woody Point Yacht Club began its official life. As a putt putt race!

'Yachts came later,' explained Beetle, who became the first handicapper for the putt putt race and stayed in the job for nearly twenty years. 'I helped Tim to buy an old yacht called *Firefly*. He restored it, started sailing, and then one day, our joke yacht club actually had a yacht race.'

'We need rules!' said Philip. And so the Woody Point Yacht Club Charter came into being with his immortal line: 'Founder members of the Woody Point Yacht Club were a dedicated group of social drinkers with a boating problem'.

In a bid to keep the club true to its highly spirited, highly eccentric beginnings, the financial section of the charter reads:

The founding members believed the club should not accumulate money, real estate or any assets of a major nature (other than a Temprite). Food and sufficient kegs are to be applied at the AGM to ensure that a zero balance is recorded by the Treasurer at the season's end. Members should contribute no more than is necessary to cover immediate and unavoidable costs, e.g. the next round. The club's only assets are the Pittwater and the warm hospitality so readily offered by members . . .

There's a prize for best-dressed boat in the annual putt putt race, but fashion ideas often take a bizarre twist as pirates and buccaneers ride the seas.

Members unable (or unwilling) to meet their financial obligations, i.e. bastards who won't pay, may, at the Committee's discretion, be threatened with Life Membership to alleviate the Treasurer's workload. Such penalty may also be applied to Members issuing worthless IOUs.

Decisions regarding the club could be made at meetings with a quorum of 'one member and one bottle of champagne' (although in times of hardship, 'a bottle of beer' would do).

When Tim Shaw, the much-loved driving force of the yacht club, was found drowned in 1988 after what is believed to be a boating accident in dreadful weather, the community fell silent in shock and grief. Bomber, one of the original group members, decided to create his own memorial to a man who'd enriched so many lives. Three times he put chains around a giant boulder, craned it onto his barge, *Trump*, and set off for Woody Point.

Three times, the chains broke and the boulders sank into the bay. The fourth time he made it and, if you look hard, there's a large stone with a plaque nailed to it in Tim's memory.

After Tim's death, Clint and David bought the putt putt and Tim's ashes were spread in Pittwater.

'Some spilt in *Pelican* so my partner, Jenny, and I reckon the odd bit of Tim might still be lodged in a crack or under a rib,' David said. When the urn was finally empty, it was put to good use as a bailer and champagne ice bucket. 'If we had a beer during a putt putt, we always poured a bit in the urn for Tim.'

CPBS N

Nowadays, from 5.30 onwards on a Wednesday afternoon, more than sixty boats jockey around the lovely timber start boat, *Percerverance*, in a race that's handicapped so that no-one ever wins the series twice.

The rule of 'anything that floats can sail' still applies and although the fleet now includes large and very flash yachts (nicknamed 'Moneyboxes' by some of us), it is the smaller, cherished vessels, timber or fibreglass, that win the hearts of the locals. And it is the gentlemanly skippers with a passion for boats, the water and a funny little yacht club that doesn't even have a clubhouse, that set the tone for the club. This is a race that has always been more about community than competition. Which is its charm. To be truthful, as the fleet has grown, it is getting more difficult to know the names of skippers and crews on every boat. And the yell for 'buoy room' at the markers is becoming far more common when, once, all we cared about was not spilling our drinks. But the spirit of the club – the larrikin, generous spirit of Tim Shaw at the very beginning – still lives on. If it falters, it's only for a moment.

The putt putt race tradition also continues and every Australia Day weekend, timber putt putts, gentleman's launches and working boats gather off Treharne Cove for a handicap start and a race around Scotland Island.

At around 10 am, boats with Australian flags flying from masts, sterns, bowsprits, shrouds and halyards chug alongside the barge to pick up numbers for their start. There are weird outfits, dogs on bows and a party spirit that surges on long after the race is over (no-one cares who wins) and we jump off our boats to swim to Treharne Cove for (another) picnic.

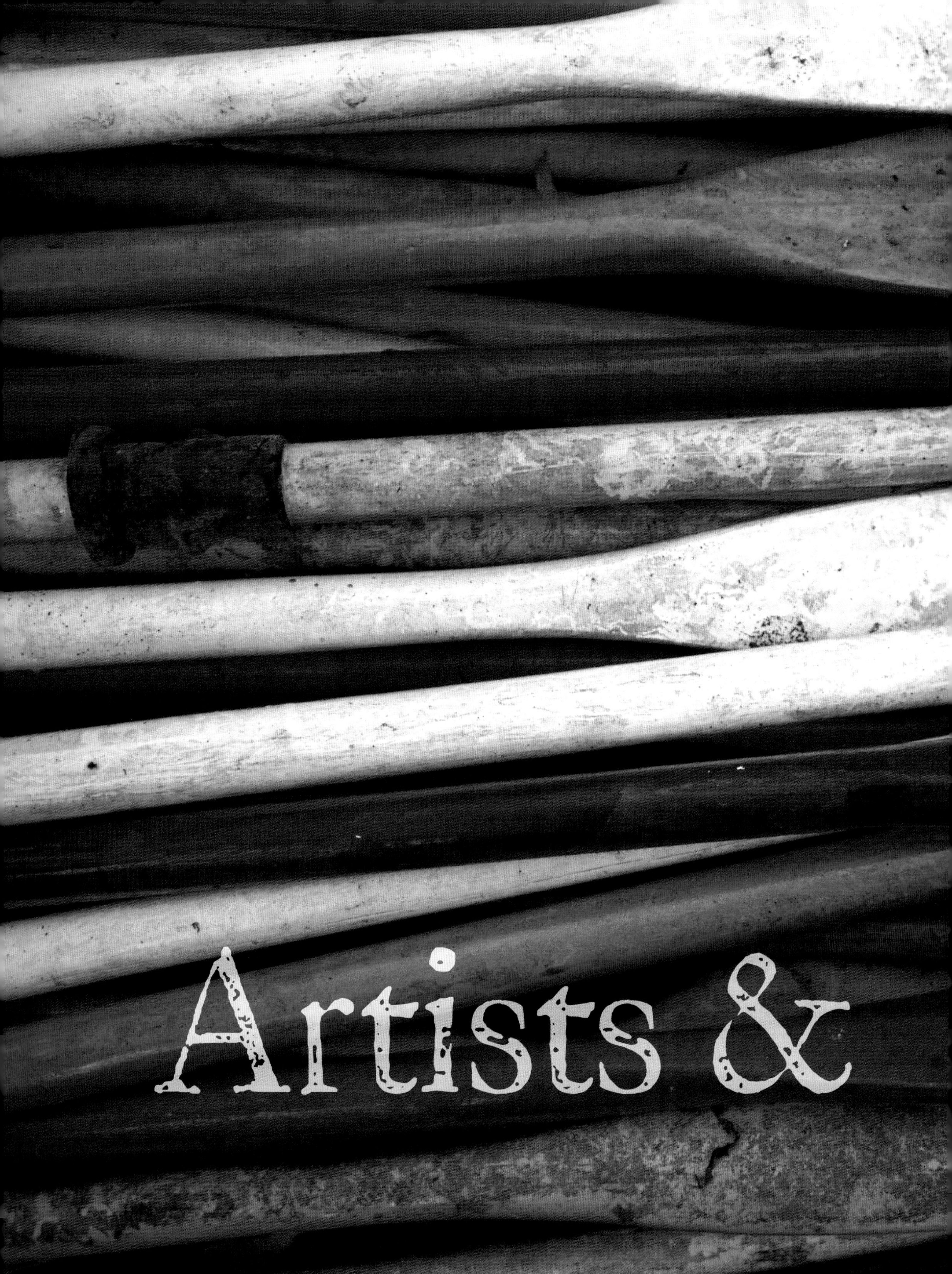
Artists &

Actors

Actors and artists, singers and songwriters – everyone's creative spirit gets a chance to shine for a moment or two in wildly colourful art shows and riotous theatrical productions.

An eclectic bunch of painters, sculptors, printers, illustrators, potters and amateur artists live on the Island and around the Bays. In fact, scratch the surface of nearly any offshore resident, and you'll find an artist of one kind or another lurking under the surface. Art is everywhere – driftwood hung with shells at the back door, old buoys strung across a deck, abandoned oars painted in vibrant colours leaning against a wall, fisherman's baskets hanging from beams – anything and everything scooped from piles of debris and resurrected to become a beautiful design.

'There's space to think here,' says prize-winning artist Tracy Smith. 'The environment suits creative souls.' For a long time, too, it was a relatively inexpensive area to live – and still within easy reach of city galleries.

Most years, a committee of artists gets together to organise an exhibition, which either takes place in the hall, the Scotland Island fire shed or, occasionally, at *Tarrangaua*. It can be a fundraising event, or purely an opportunity for artists to show and sell their

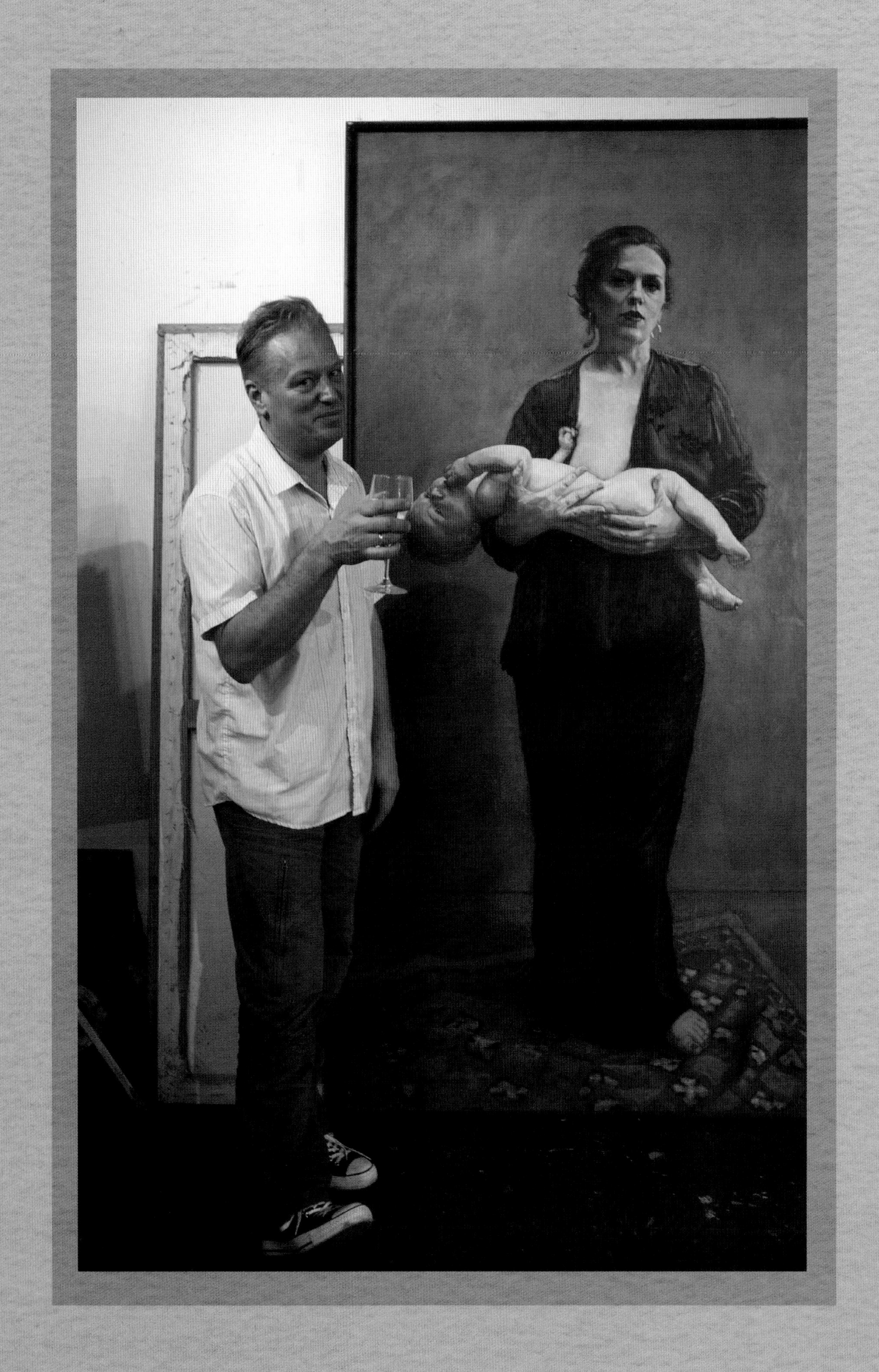

Dimitri Lihachov with his portrait of his wife and child in his large Scotland Island studio.

work. Mostly it's a combination of both. A bucket gets plonked at the front door asking for contributions to the fire brigade, the kindergarten or any worthy local projects. A percentage of sales are often donated and there's rarely any hesitation when an artist is asked to create a work for a charity auction.

Art exhibitions are notoriously difficult to mount, even under ideal circumstances. Add boats, weather and water into the equation and the potential for disaster escalates dramatically. It doesn't seem to bother anyone though. Huge canvasses are loaded into tiny, tippy tinnies, precious pottery is wrapped and boxed for transport, sculpture installations are gently dismantled and laid, bit by bit, on barges. Then it's all shipped across the water, with fingers crossed tightly on the tiller of the outboard motor. And, occasionally, a wad of gauze plugging a small leak in the hull.

In November 2005, the Island H'Arts held an exhibition at *Tarrangaua*. After a series of meetings in the Smiths' boatshed, details were nutted out and the committee given their allotted tasks. The day before the opening, as light drizzle turned to gentle rain, tinnies stacked with plastic-wrapped canvasses began arriving at the Lovett Bay ferry wharf.

Meanwhile, the bagged walls of *Tarrangaua* were stripped bare, the verandah floor polished, the windows cleaned and the fridge filled with food to make sandwiches for hungry visitors. Earlier in the month, lemon cakes, apricot slices and chocolate brownies had been baked and frozen for morning and afternoon teas. All proceeds were destined for the Western Foreshores Volunteer Bush Fire Brigade and yellow-suited fireys served tea and coffee in shifts over the whole weekend. They also helped visitors up and down the eighty-eight steps when necessary and coordinated the ferry trips.

Visiting artist Tim Storrier opened the show on a brilliantly sunny day to a full house. The cash register began to ring joyfully. The bucket filled with donations, and ticket sales to win a linocut print of a Pittwater scene donated by artist Katie Clemson soared. We had a hit on our hands.

Previous page: Rouge Hoffman at her pottery wheel, and artist Jack Vaughan's wonderful studio. Left: Artist, author and children's book illustrator, Nettie Lodge. Above, from left: Illustrator Gwyn Perkins who drew the map of the bays for this book, artist Marion van den Driesschen, master printer Paul Smith and artist Tracy Smith.

Art exhibitions are fraught with danger when work has to be shipped in leaky tin dinghies on wet and windy days.

Then the next day, the heavens opened, the wind swung round to shoot straight from the Antarctic and blasted directly onto the verandah. The damp brought out leeches that hung alongside the steps waiting to pounce. No-one, we thought, will venture out in this kind of weather. But people did. The verandah rails were hung with wet weather gear like limp flags, and shoes and boots started to pile high at the front door. Umbrellas were stuffed into a garbage bin. A tarpaulin was hung at one end of the verandah to protect the cakes from the rain, and sales of red wine labels (attached to a free bottle of wine) took off. 'Medicinal,' everyone chirped, 'to warm us up.'

Artists may come and go – the number living offshore ranges between twenty-five and almost fifty at any given time – but their joy in their work and their generosity of spirit makes them one of the strong, underlying linchpins of our offshore community. They enrich our lives.

Fireys serve afternoon tea.

The verandah becomes an art gallery.

Pottery is carried by hand.

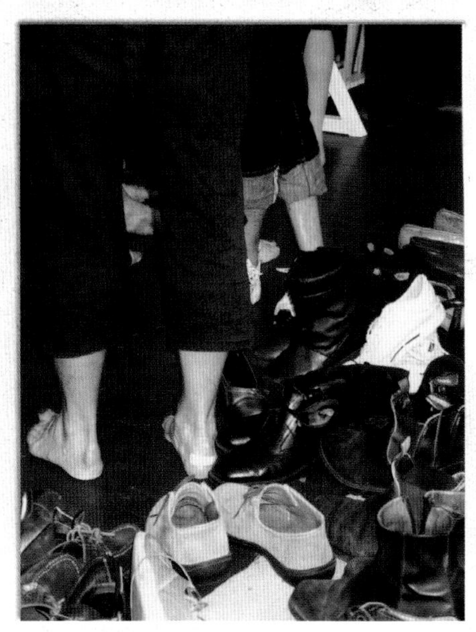

Wet shoes pile up when the rain falls.

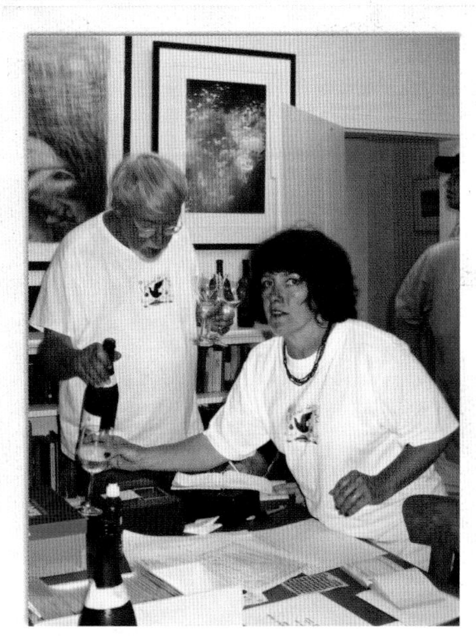

Working out the financial details.

Artworks arrive by tinny.

Loading the truck for the uphill trip.

Hanging art is a tricky business.

Umbrellas are stored haphazardly.

the rocky horror show

November 2007

live at the scotland island community hall

Actors often pay so little attention to the script that if you go to a performance more than once you could be forgiven for thinking it was a new play with the same set.

From the first days of Madame Stephanie, an Italian concert pianist who built a stage in her home at *Trincomalee*, enthusiastic singers, writers and musicians have banded together to make their own entertainment. A singalong around the piano, a recital by anyone who could play a musical instrument, or a few slapstick skits referring to local events.

By the 1970s, productions had become a little more sophisticated and were performed in the basement of Laurie Duff's (the ferry driver) home. The ensemble of anyone with the energy and the time soon became known as the Scotland Island Players, a name that has stuck.

As productions became more ambitious, residents asked the council (then Warringah although it is now Pittwater) to fund a community hall. Each request was knocked back – building offshore was considered too difficult and despite more people living on the island, the numbers were still too small to justify the expense. In the end, according to long-time Scotland Island resident and one of the guiding forces behind the project, Bob Blackwood, the community offered to build the hall if the council paid for materials. Work began in 1980 with volunteer weekend labour. The building was completed in 1982 at a total cost of $20,000 and promptly insured for $120,000. It is now the most important public asset on the island. Plays, art exhibitions, fundraisers, birthday parties, musical soirees, yoga classes – just about anything – take place in the hall where a large commemorative tapestry, made by local women, hangs on the wall.

Over the years, a huge diversity of theatre has been enthusiastically performed. Some written by locals, others borrowed from professional playwrights. 'It was quite common to get a script from the library and then photocopy it,' Bob said, grinning. 'Write a few of our own lines, too, to make it more relevant to island life.' The process worked well but came unstuck when the group 'borrowed' from 'Table Manners' from *The Norman Conquests* by British playwright Alan Ayckborn.

'We had quite a successful season – sell-outs – over two weekends,' Bob recalled. Then a large manila envelope arrived for the show's producer/director/referee.

'In the corner, the sender's name was listed as Alan Ayckborn Productions,' Bob said. 'We'd been caught! We all thought we were going to lose our homes. The producer was packing death.'

Filled with fear, he opened the envelope. There was a photo of the author. On it he'd written 'Best Wishes to the Scotland Island Players. Carry on the good work'. Apparently, some friends of Ayckborn's had seen the poster on one of the ferry wharves and sent it to him with a note saying that he was now so famous his work was performed as far away as the Antipodes.

'Ayckborn was thrilled.'

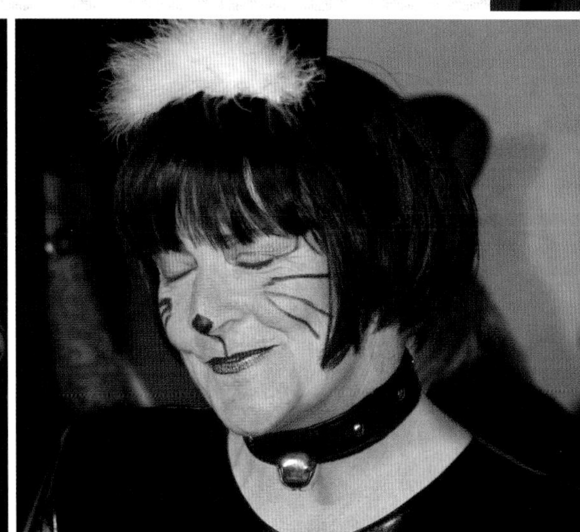

The Players have one other distinction. It is apparently the only amateur company in the world that has ever been given permission to perform *The Rocky Horror Show*.

'Perseverance,' Bob said. 'A Scotland Islander, Jon Hazelwood, was involved with the Sydney production of the show. He kept pestering the copyright holders until he got a yes.'

Performances by the Scotland Island Players, which usually run over the Friday and Saturday of successive weekends, are wonderfully unruly. Like stepping into country town life fifty years ago. The audience and the players are neighbours, sometimes the ad libs are funnier than the script, and no-one has expectations beyond having fun. The bigger the fool you make of yourself, the more you're appreciated. The audience brings a picnic and a bottle or two of wine and sometimes the family dog. Cakes are shared, sandwiches offered around and every so often, a member of the production team, wearing pancake makeup, black fishnet stockings and a Playboy bunny outfit, wanders around with a platter of cheese and bikkies.

Once, a classical music recital was given in an acoustically brilliant cave in Frog Hollow, a pretty little rainforest inlet in Lovett Bay. A grand piano was lowered from the house until it fitted snugly under the rock overhang where, no doubt, for hundreds and even thousands of years, Aborigines from the Guringai tribe took shelter. People passing in tinnies heard the music, cut their engines and threw out anchors to listen while the water rocked them and the moon rose on the horizon.

The

Dog Race

The entry fee is a long neck bottle of beer – and a can of dog food. Winner takes all!

Every Christmas Eve, in heatwaves or gales, dogs, kids, locals and visitors happily gather at The Point for the wonderfully chaotic Scotland Island to Church Point Dog Race and to wish each other the best of the season.

Dogs. Tall. Short. Lean. Plump. Fluffy. Sleek. Smart. And sometimes a little bit slow on the uptake. They are an integral part of Pittwater life. They ride the bows of tinnies like furry figureheads, spend hot lazy days lolling on jetties, or hang out with their owners at The Point when work is over for the day. They hover at dinner parties, know which guest is a certainty to pass a tidbit under the table, and if you go away for a few days, someone always offers to mind them. Most dogs are so familiar with everyone's homes they know where every stash of bones is buried in every backyard.

Every Christmas Eve, there's a dog race that begins at Bell Wharf on Scotland Island and ends on the little sandy beach at the Church Point ferry wharf. The race goes on no matter what – gales, torrential rain or a heatwave. The community turns up to watch as forty-odd dogs paddle their way to a place in local legend. None of us will ever forget Diesel, a leggy black dog smarter than most humans, who won three times. When he died, his owner, Benny, created a new trophy for best local dog and called it the Diesel King trophy. An earlier trophy, donated by former Scotland Island resident and Mona Vale vet, Robert Bradley, disappeared after an onshore dog won it.

... boats, dogs, people and a party spirit on Christmas Eve ...

NO TIE
UP AREA
ADA882N

On Christmas Eve, we all make our way in our tinnies to The Point from about five o'clock onwards with picnic baskets, ice-boxes, blankets and our hounds. And a can of dog food and a long-neck bottle of beer, which is the entry fee if your dog is racing. The first people to arrive – usually families with oldies in tow – pick prime positions along the seawall and settle in with camp chairs and a table for the cheese, bikkies and bottle of wine. They are immovable. Even when a dog fight threatens to knock them all into the bay. The rest of us wander happily, waving Merry Christmas, touching base like family as the final days of the old year segue into the new.

Dogs at our feet. Panting. Piddling. Dozing. Slobbering. Standing. Leaning. Or snarling if some mutt runs off with another mutt's ball.

It's all deliciously laidback. People in sarongs, swimmers, grubby T-shirts. A few white linen shirts here and there, but not enough to change the atmosphere from gloriously and unabashedly hick to nouveau swish. We may be part of the city of Sydney but we are a country town in spirit.

For the last few years, the race has been organised by Russ and Scotty. At about five o'clock, a registration point with a banner appears under a tree. Owners roll up with the entry fee, and the dog's name gets added to a list on a bit of paper. As the scheduled start time of six o'clock draws closer, animals and their owners are ferried from The Point to Bell Wharf in a relay of tinnies until they're all assembled on the shore. The race begins when the starter gun goes off. Scotty, who does the ferrying to Bell Wharf, races back to the beach to grab the winners. Owners can swim, paddle or row with their dogs but no motors are allowed.

Every dog is a star in his owner's eyes but gets a chance to be a hero for a day in the hilarious annual dog race.

… and the race is on!
Owners and dogs churn the water as they race
to the finish line …

RIP CURL

The crowd cheers wildly as the winning dog paddles to glory and a place in local history, with his owner urging him on for the final few yards.

The origins of the dog race are murky. The most common memory is that when there were two ferry services competing hotly for local business (a co-op formed by local residents tired of feeling hostage to a single service, and a privately owned service) both drivers, naturally, had a dog. During a heated discussion one evening, the drivers challenged each other to a race. A dog race. When locals heard about it, everyone with a dog wanted to take part. Memories are hazy about the first year it took place, and Pittwater being Pittwater, there are many versions of the event. Most agree it began about thirty years ago.

At the time of writing, only one other dog holds a record to match Diesel's. Minnie. She's a tiny black-and-white fox terrier with an independent spirit and a huge heart. Her record stands at three too. For coming last. On Pittwater, the triers – anyone that faces down the odds with a glint in an eye and a bucket of courage – are always given their moment to shine.

Spectators line the shore, the ferry wharf, climb onto the fire escape of the *Pasadena* or hover offshore in boats like a navy of dinghies. They watch as black, brown, brindled, white or tan heads get closer and closer. When the dogs emerge from the water, there's a roar from the crowd. The winner shakes. Water sprays everywhere. The grannies are drenched but they still don't budge. The party continues long after the last little doggy has hit the beach to a final cheer – and a prize for coming last, which is usually a dog bowl. The dogs are the heroes of the day. They bask in the glory, then ride home proudly, their front paws on the bow. Noble, in a mutt way. Tinnies and dogs.

Quintessential Pittwater. 

Last Word

I have lived on Pittwater for ten years now. Physically, not a lot has changed since my first boat ride in 1999 to see a house for sale. There are still five homes and the working boatshed in our little nook at the mouth of Salvation Creek. And although bushfires have threatened from time to time, we have so far been spared, sometimes only at the last minute, by a sea breeze kicking in and turning back the flames.

Lovett Bay has a new ferry wharf now. Pale blue and built with a shelter for the garbage bins so that strong winds won't send them spilling into the water. We mourned the loss of our old leaning shed with its broken windows and gaps in the timber, but really, this is far more practical and comfortable. The old seawall, at least, remains. Coated in a new slab of concrete that the kids couldn't resist writing their names on. Mallee. Isaac. Aero. Ek. Vincent. Lucia.

In 2008, the five-year drought finally let go of its grip on the land. The bush lifted its head after the first heavy downpour and, in a moment, we all forgot the dusty and bleached, flattened landscape of the dry years. Salvation Creek never stopping flowing, though, little more than a trickle at the worst times, but still there. Aptly named.

Each morning, before the wind kicks in and if the tide is high, kayakers glide silently past the mangroves. The Lovett Bay boatshed opens for business. The kids rush to catch the school ferry. The rest of us go about our daily life in what I like to think is an easily measured pace that leaves time for long moments just sitting and watching the physical world unfold with its ever-changing stories.

There is not a single day that I do not say a silent thank-you for the privilege of living here. Each day feels like a gift.

Perhaps because it is.

Acknowledgements

Many thanks to all the wonderful offshore residents – our big-hearted community – who were so kind about sharing their time, stories and local knowledge. Their generosity of spirit is one of the many reasons the Scotland Island and Western Foreshores is a truly rich community. Thank-you, too, to everyone who gave his and her time to be photographed and to dig out old material to remind us of how each generation that came here added another layer to our way of life.

The glorious pictures in this book speak for themselves, but I'd really like to add special thanks to Anthony Ong for seeing the beauty of battered tinnies, leaning boatsheds and the ragged bush. The Bays and Scotland Island are not, and never have been, about glamour. They are about our quirky, vibrant, eclectic and never-dull locals who don't give a damn what kind of car you drive, only whether you're a good neighbour. Anthony has captured that so beautifully.

Thanks to Alana Landsberry for stepping in to photograph the Woody Point Yacht Club Putt Putt Day at such short notice. She did a fantastic job under difficult conditions. Thanks, too, to Scotland Island photographer June Lahm who captures random Pittwater moments beautifully and truthfully and is a great chronicler of local life. Then there's Gwyn Perkins – a man who sees the world with a rare combination of wisdom and innocence, which shines through his art. Thanks, Gwynnie, for the map. It's a treasure.

I'm grateful to Nick Reeve, Bernice Dunn, Beth Franklin, Marty Cowan, Nick Cowdery and Sophie Wilson, who took the time to search through their old photo albums for pictures of the 1994 bushfires. Thanks to Jenny Winterton for her terrific pictures of the volunteer fire brigade Pittwater back-burns.

Thanks to Kerry Borthwick, Bob Bolton and Bob Blackwood for digging in their archives to find old Scotland Island Players programmes. Thanks to Prue Sky, Sandy Cozens and David Yardley for their invaluable input and local knowledge about the earlier days and for taking the time to set straight some misty moments of local history.

Thanks to publisher Nikki Christer, who had the courage to take on this project, and Jill Brown, who understood the challenges of photographing *Tarrangaua*. Thanks to Liz Seymour who made the book come alive and Ingrid Korda for her finessing.

Thank you, too, to my friend, neighbour and agent, Caroline Adams. Her tact, wisdom, local knowledge and quiet understanding at every stage of the project were – as usual – pure gold.

Finally, thanks to my husband, Bob. He makes everything possible with his love, support, encouragement . . . and patience!

Contacts

There are various types of accommodation available in the area.

Pittwater YHA at Towlers Bay (also known as Morning Bay) can be accessed via ferry or water taxi from Church Point to Halls Wharf, where there is a signposted, uphill walk to the hostel, situated within the Ku-ring-gai Chase National Park.

Ph: 61 2 9999 5748
Website: www.yha.com.au
Email: Pittwater@yhansw.org.au

The Scotland Island Lodge, Scotland Island, accessed via ferry or water taxi from Church Point, has two double guest rooms and includes breakfast in the tariff. Other meals can be organised on request.

Ph: 61 2 9979 3301
or bookings at info@scotlandislandlodge.com

Two real estate agents specialise in local property sales, rentals and holiday lettings:
Tanya Mottl, Century 21 Showcase Pittwater, Bayview Anchorage Marina, 10a/1714 Pittwater Road, Bayview NSW 2104.

Ph: 61 2 9999 0155
Mobile: 0411 113 317
Website: www.c21pittwater.com.au

Melanie & John Marshall, PMC Hill Real Estate, Shop 2/1858 Pittwater Road, Church Point, NSW 2105.

Ph: 61 2 9999 4902
Mobile: 0415 440 662
Website: www.pmchill.com.au

For ferry charter, contact Penny Gleen at the Church Point Ferry Service.

Ph: 0433 038 408
Website: www.churchpointferryservice.com
Email: penny@churchpointferryservice.com

Photo credits

All photographs are by Anthony Ong except for:
Caroline Adams, p.51
Nick Reeve, p.54
Sophie Wilson, p.54
Jenny Winterton, p.55
Alana Landsberry, p.84–5, 88, 92, 96, 196–7, 198–9, 201, 202, 203
June Lahm, p.94–5, 154, 183, 189, 214, 215, 216, 218–9, 237
Bob Story, p.146
Ken Griffiths, p.147
Tanya Mottle, p.176 (bottom left & centre), 179 (top & bottom right)

Photos in *The Pledge* are from the family albums of Prue Sky.

An Ebury Press book
Published by Random House Australia Pty Ltd
Level 3, 100 Pacific Highway, North Sydney NSW 2060
www.randomhouse.com.au

First published by Ebury Press in 2009

Addresses for companies within the Random House Group can be found at
www.randomhouse.com.au/offices

National Library of Australia
Cataloguing-in-Publication Entry

Duncan, Susan (Susan Elizabeth).
A life on Pittwater.

ISBN: 978 1 74166 669 4 (hbk).

Duncan, Susan (Susan Elizabeth).
Women journalists – Australia – Biography.
Dwellings – New South Wales – Pittwater.
Pittwater (NSW).

920.72

Cover photography by Anthony Ong
Cover and internal design by MaryLouise Brammer
Additional internal design and layout by Seymour Designs
Printed and bound by Imago in China

Random House Australia uses papers that are natural, renewable and recyclable
products and made from wood grown in sustainable forests. The logging and
manufacturing processes are expected to conform to the environmental regulations
of the country of origin.

10 9 8 7 6 5 4 3 2 1

Towlers Bay
Halls
Lovett Bay
Lovett